Economic Thoughts and Principles of Management in the Shantiparva of the Mahabharata

Economic Thoughts and Principles of Management in the Shantiparva of the Mahabharata

Dr. Mousumi Ghosh

AUTHORSPRESS

Worldwide Circulation through Authorspress Global Network
First Published in 2021
by
Authorspress
Q-2A Hauz Khas Enclave, New Delhi-110 016 (India)
Phone: (0) 9818049852
E-mail: authorspressgroup@gmail.com
Website: www.authorspressbooks.com

Economic Thoughts and Principles of Management in the Shantiparva of the Mahabharata
ISBN 978-93-91314-20-0

Printed in India at Thomson Press (India) Limited

Foreword

Though a challenging task, it is with immense pleasure that I accepted the request of Dr. Mousumi Ghosh to write a foreword to her illuminating book *Economic Thoughts and Principles of Management in The Shantiparva of The Mahabharata.* Of all the books I have read and taught *The Mahabharata* is the one which I love most and influenced me considerably in my philosophic thoughts, way of life and writings. Dr. Mousumi Ghosh has been in close contact with me for several years as a patron member of Guild of Indian English Writers, Editors and Critics (GIEWEC), of which I am the Secretary and Editor in Chief. She has been publishing her outstanding research papers on contemporary Economic theories and practices in both our journals *Writers Editors Critics* (WEC) and *International Journal on Multicultural Literature* (IJML). Humble, simple, loving and erudite personality, Dr. Mousumi, motivated by her multitalented renowned philosopher-writer guru, Dr. Ramesh Chandra Mukhopadhyaya, has already published several books and innumerable research papers in her discipline, Economics.

The author has divided the book into five chapters followed by a long list of bibliography. The first chapter is the Introduction by which Dr. Mousumi introduces Shantiparva, Mahabharata, Vedas etc. to the readers. In her own words, "The Shantiparva of the Mahabharata is discourse and thoughts on peace. The longest epic tale, the Mahabharata needs no introduction. The Shantiparva is the twelfth of the eighteen books of the Mahabharata. It is the longest among all and consists of 365 chapters and 13,716 slokas or verses." She goes on in detail and tells about the three sub books or Parvas of the Shantiparva – Rajadharma anushaasana Parva, Apaddharma anushaasana Parva and Mokshadharma Parva. Mousumi is of opinion that "literature as such holds the mirror to a society. And no wonder that an epic of the Mahabharata size seems to hold out a mirror to the different aspects of the society and thoughts that were prevalent in India of the time in which it was composed. Since in absence of other evidences, literature itself is a source of history, we hereby seek to decode economic thoughts and economic activity of the Mahabharata age." Kurukshetra war seems to be the most catastrophic war in the world where warriors from different countries assembled to fight either on behalf of the Pandavas or on the behalf of Kauravas. Mousumi writes that it has been something like a world war and greater in its intensity than the two world wars that the world has witnessed of late. The total number of men directly killed in the second Great War has been 50-56 million and the total number of Kshatriyas killed in the Kurukshetra war which lasted only for eighteen days was one billion, six hundred and sixty million and twenty thousand men. The conflict between Pandavas and Kauravas was centred around some acres of land. The author argues that eonomics of any particular society is dependent on the political substructure of the society. At the same time the political substructure of the society is dependent on the economic substructure of the society. Hence she ventures in the book to explore the economic thought and activity and political thought and activity of the Mahabharata age that are commingled. The ultimate objective of mankind is peace and this book is a study of how economic activities coupled with right management principles can give peace.

Mousumi has adopted a new methodology in the book. An interdisciplinary study of economics and literature needs a deep searching of economic ideas within literature and literature within economics. The Mahabharata, a genre of literature itself, depicted a society, the Mahabharata society. The Shantiparva is viewed as an alternative socio-economic thought with its own ethics, culture, socio economic outlook, management principles and administrative norms that might apply in the world today with success. Thus, it is also a search for the epistemology of economics.

Dr. Mousumi has taken a herculean task of condensing the thoughts of the gigantic Shantiparva into this small book. She has pointed out the recurrent motifs in the Shantiparva. They are – the Vedic ideas of charity, the caste system Chaturvarna and its economic implications, the four phases of human life known as chaturashram, symbolised as the code of righteous living, treasury and wealth in management, the significance of right time and distribution of surplus, Yajna, duties of a king, public finance, fiscal and monetary policies, public governance system, Dandaniti or justice, dharma or righteous living norms, rights, justice, prosperity and welfare of the people, and the subject of moksha or spiritual liberation through proper observance of righteous socio economic prescribed norms. What a thorough research the author has made is visible in the table she has added in the chapter which displayed the frequency of occurrence of specific words in the text Shatiparva. The table consists of 36 specific words with a frequency of occurrence from minimum 2 to maximum 219. For example the word 'Wealth' occurs in 219 places and 'Dharma' in 195. A glimpse at the frequency distribution table, even without any deep reading of the chapter, gives an idea of the discourse. The concept of wealth, righteousness or dharma, money, Yajna the sacrifice rituals, punishment or Dandaniti, the use of sceptre to protect righteousness, desires, ethics, cow as wealth, gift, donations, taxes, peace are some notable themes of economics and management. Mousumi argues that the economic thoughts in ancient India are found in the four Vedas. It is the economics of abundance, not the western concept of economics of scarcity. The Vedas and the Upanishads are sources for the theoretical framework of ancient Indian economics and the Shantiparva contains the guidelines to live a life in that way that is described in various forms.

Chapter two is the discussion on the Mahabharata and the Vedic society. Dr. Mousumi writes, "The Vedic civilisation has been the fountainhead of Indian civilisation of the epic age. The two great epics the Ramayana and the Mahabharata mentioned innumerable times about the Vedic rishis, the poet philosophers of the Vedic times and their teachings. The Vedas are the oldest scriptures and the earliest documents of the human knowledge. The four books of the Vedas are Rig, Sama, Yajur and Atharva. The Vedas in a nutshell consist of the hymns, ritualistic texts and guidelines on sacrificial duties. However, they are the repositories of spiritual knowledge embedded in all aspects of human life, mostly the religious, social, economic and political ones. As time wore on, from one Veda four Vedas grew, and their interpretations assumed the name of the fifth Veda, for the common people, as the Bharata Samhita, which afterwards developed into the great Indian epics, the Mahabharata and the Ramayana. The Mahabharata is said to be fifth Veda. To give examples of the elements of economics and how the Mahabharata society had been evolved from the Vedic society, we can refer to the Chaturvarna, chaturashrama and the chaturvarga. Constraints of space compel me to not go in detail on this chapter.

Chapter three is entitled "Cow – A Wealth in the Ancient Indian Literature and Archetypal in Present Indian Literature." The chapter is an attempt to find the deeper meaning of wealth in cow. Cows were given to Brahmins as dakshina, the voluntary payment after a Brahmin performed any ritual. Wealth has many functions to perform. But greed for wealth often leads to disaster. Yudhisthira lamented that for greed of wealth and power, they had killed their own friends. He wanted to sacrifice all his material wealth and the desire for the same. Arjuna sought to change his elder brother's attitude towards material wealth. He advised his brother that his duty was to organise Yajna, the sacrificial ceremony for distribution of wealth.

Cow is the most important economic wealth in ancient India. Among the sources of livelihood described there, cows played significant roles. Not only the Arthashastra, since the days of the Vedas, the whole gamut of literature especially the epics the Ramayana and the Mahabharata are loud with the praise of cow. Mousumi continues, "The ancient Indian philosophers, the Vedic rishis and their progenies were conscious not only of the human inhabitants of the mother earth but also of all the living creatures and the environment. They advised people to learn the way of living by observing the way of living of other creatures, specially the cows in many contexts. No doubt with this unclouded insight, they could declare: 'Just as the cows love their calves, you too love each other'". The earliest stage of civilisation is taken to be the hunting stage. As the hunting age passes to the pastoral and animals are domesticated, the animal itself, not its skin, becomes the unit of value. The most common of such animals in India is the cow which is mentioned in the Rigveda. Cows provided major source of revenue for the government. The possibility of herdsmen starving calves of their mother's milk was foreseen, milking cows twice in seasons when they should be milked only once was punished by cutting off the thumb of the culprit, killing or inducing someone to kill animals in cow herds were punishable by death. Special provisions were made for looking after nonproductive cattle. The cow is a recurrent motif in the Mahabharata. The society depicted in the Mahabharata is agrarian. Cattle and land are the major components of wealth in a kingdom. Cattle theft is a common theme in the Mahabharata. Moreover, references to pastoral lands being included in forest areas and cattle expeditions for counting cows and branding calves are included in the Mahabharata. The name of the cow is mentioned at least thirty times in different contexts in the Shantiparva. Cow in the Mahabharata is an indicator of good governance. Mousumi writes, "When there is good government the environment becomes such that nature including plants and animals seem to bless us with plenty. And surely cow was the wealth in the then society of the Ramayana and the Mahabharata because it was the major source of livelihood for many." The importance of cow and other animals on earth and the necessity of man's cohabitance with nonhuman beings is portrayed beautifully by Dr. Mousumi through the explication of K. V. Dominic's poem "A Cow on the Lane" which has reference to the Mahabharata and the Ramayana.

The author then writes on treasury and wealth in management. The great Patriarch of the Kaurava clan Bhisma gave advice to Yudhisthira in the Shantiparva, the chapter on peace. Yudhisthira, obeying the advice of Lord Krishna, requested the knowledgeable Bhisma about the duties of a king and the management of the state. Bhisma stated that without the four principles of human object Dharma the righteousness, Artha the material wealth, Kama the passion and Moksha the spiritual wisdom, the purpose of a king cannot be accomplished only with what is lotted. Mousumi goes on explaining, "The Sanatana Dharma or the Universal Righteous duty according to Bhisma is acquisition of wealth, its careful protection and the augmentation of that wealth and property. He did not recommend any extreme to do that. A ruler should not acquire wealth only by cruelty or only by honesty. A combination of civility and cruelty is necessary for the collection of wealth for the treasury. A weak ruler cannot acquire wealth, and, the wealthless person is a weak one. A weak ruler cannot rule for long. The Shantiparva draws an illustration that like clothes which covers private parts of a body of a woman, wealth and property of a king covers all his sins."

The title of Chapter Four is "The Necessity of a Ruler – The Socio-Economic Perspectives of the Shantiparva of the Mahabharata." The great Indian epics, the Ramayana and the Mahabharata dwell elaborately on the necessity of an efficient king, the ideal state and governance. Ram Rajya, the kingdom of Shri Rama is referred to as a model one even today when one speaks what is meant by a peaceful state. Ram Rajya in the Ramayana society is referred to as an ideal society where everybody follows a code of righteous living and everybody is more or less happy, getting all their essential needs. Dr. Mousumi explains, "There are three qualities in man – Sattva, Rajas and Tamas. While Sattva is light and while it is open and above board, tamas is heavy and dark. Tamas strives to hide everything. Between these two poles, Rajas moves to and fro. In this context we can surmise that the majority of the people of a state goaded by greed and corruption remains underdeveloped. It is the Rajas the Raja or the rulers who must charge the idle folk with vitality and economic activity with a view to pursuing dharma, artha, kama, moksha." Bhisma in the Shantiparva has highlighted the need for government for protection of private property. Without protection from the king, the head of the state in the Mahabharata society, no one can have any possession over anything on earth, be it over his wife, children, food and other consumables or over any other materials. Without security from a king, all wealth ultimately perishes. When a king protects his citizens, the citizens of all Varnas engage in different economic activities, perform Yajnas and rituals for gods and concentrate on their studies. The ritual of Yajna is designed to establish man's connection with the cosmic properties abounding in the universe. Mousumi concludes the chapter thus: "Bhisma's discourse on the necessity of a king is based widely on the economic grounds. Without an effective government, the creation, preservation and proper distribution of wealth cannot take place. The lust for wealth brings the consequences like lawlessness, war, hamper of economic activities like trade, agriculture and cow rearing. And the most important of all is that the Yajna or the ritualistic sacrifice, the foundation of the Mahabharata society could not be possible without the supervision of the king."

Chapter Five consists of some notes on Shantiparva. On Biksha or begging Mousumi notes that in India's spiritual tradition, begging or Bhiksha was a way of seeking spiritual wealth. And spiritual wealth which is search for liberation or moksha is the ultimate freedom from worldly bondages. The ancient Indian literatures especially the Ramayana and the Mahabharata do not consider begging as a hateful activity. Begging indicates the importance of charity in India's sociology and economic system. A human being is not always a selfish rational person with its own bundle of worldly demands. He has some altruistic desires. Giving alms is a way of fulfilling that desire. Again begging also teaches an alternative way of living. It is how to live without any option of worldly choice of what to eat or drink. One is not constrained by the pressure of nonsense abundance of choices. There are such twenty-eight notes in this chapter explaining the key terms, practices and actions in the Shantiparva. The long bibliography at the end of the book shows how extensively and deeply the author has researched before writing this book.

In addition to Veda Vyasa, Dr. Mousumi has referred to in this book both ancient and modern philosophers like Plato, Aristotle, Confucius, Panini, Kautilya, Xenophon, Machiavelli, Rousseau, Maxmuller, Thomas Hobbes, Dr. S. Radhakrishnan, Adam Smith, etc. Since The Mahabharata is also a classic of literature, Mousumi has made a comparative reference to its themes and messages in the works of William Shakespeare, William Wordsworth, John Keats, P. B. Shelley, Henry David Thoreau and K. V. Dominic. Let me wind up this foreword reinstating once again that this book of Dr. Mousumi Ghosh is a gem addition to the critical and philosophical books on the Mahabharata. Hearty Congratulations dear Dr. Mousumi Ghosh!

Prof. Dr. K. V. Dominic,
English Writer and Editor

Preface

Although on the surface, economics has been an emergent discipline showing up in the wake of the eighteenth century, the study of economics is as old as ancient Indian civilisation. The present treatise seeks to retrieve the economic thoughts of ancient India showing their utility in the world today.

Our recollection of the sublime thoughts of the Shantiparva, Mahabharata might not only help our society to realise the collective thought of the nation as they are, but also this discovery of our national self could move us the nation, on the road to development, freedom and happiness.

I am greatly indebted to Dr. Ramesh Chandra Mukhopadhyaya, renowned scholar and a retired teacher of B. B. College Asansol, for his constant encouragement, able guidance and innovative suggestions, which have given me strength in every stage of the work. He is undoubtedly my mentor in Mahabharata studies and helped me to develop the alternative thought processes while carrying out my project. The useful time spent in intellectual discussions is unforgettable experiences, which will ever remain fresh in my memory.

I am grateful to the Indian English Poet and Scholar K.V. Dominic. His foreword to this book has added untold wealth to its content. I am equally grateful to the poet publisher of Authorspress. I believe that the memory of gratitude is not best served by the list of people or places that acknowledgments can account. And I must bow my head in respect to the Almighty God for giving me this opportunity to study the Mahabharata.

Whether gold is pure or whether it has any alloy could be best understood in the flames of our intellectual readers who are overflowing with compassion.

Om Tat Sat

Mousumi Ghosh

Contents

1

Introduction

Shanti, translated in English, is Peace. The Shantiparva of the Mahabharata is discourse and thoughts on peace. The longest epic tale, the Mahabharata needs no introduction. The Shantiparva is the twelfth of the eighteen books of the Mahabharata. It is the longest among all and consists of 365 chapters and 13,716 slokas or verses. It is the wealth of thoughts of the greatest intellectuals who were eminent personalities in the society of the Mahabharata. The present treatise as the title itself indicates seeks to explore the economic thoughts and the management principles of the Mahabharata Shantiparva, if any, laden in the Shantiparva Mahabharata. To that end it will not be out of place to discuss the importance of the Mahabharata and the Shantiparva in the ancient Indian literature. The Mahabharata is a vast literary work consisting of one lakh shlokas or one lakhfyttes. And it is a vast epic. Rather it is deemed as an epic of growth. We Indians believe that one person named Veda Vyasa composed it but scholars think that there have been many Vyasas who contributed to this epic through the ages. Vyasa is a central and revered figure among the ancient Indian philosophers. He is also sometimes called Veda Vyāsa the one who divided the Vedas into four parts.

The Vishnu Purana has a theory about Vyasa. The Vishnu Purana (Book 3, Ch. 3) says: "Twenty-eight times have the

Vedas been arranged by the great rishis in the *Vaivasvata Manvantara...* and consequently eight and twenty Vyasas have passed away; by whom, in the respective periods, the Veda has been divided into four" (https://en.wikipedia.org/wiki/Vyasa). But for our purpose we assume that the Mahabharata is a text composed by Vyasa the son of Parasara.

There is lot of debate among the scholars as to the exact date of compilation of the Mahabharata. As stated by Maurice Winternitz, the German Indologist "the Mahabharata cannot have received its present form earlier than the 4th century BC and not later than the 4th century AD" (Winternitz, p. 465). A. Macdonell states that the epic must have acquired its present character by about 350 AD (Mahabharata: Its status and retellings, Chapter II, shodhganga.inflibnet.ac.in).

And surely the Mahabharata is the summit of the literary tradition and the traditions set forth by the Vedas. While the Vedas are unanimously accepted by the scholars of all ages as the most ancient treatises of knowledge, there have been differences in assessment of the period of their origin. According to ancient Indian scriptures and sages, the Vedas are as old as Nature because they represent the divine voice, which emerged at the time of the Creation of Nature.

Among the western scholars, Prof. F. Maxmuller (in the *History of Ancient Sanskrit Literature*, p. 244) estimates their period to be somewhere in-between 1500 to 1200 years B.C. However, his views were not acceptable to many of his contemporary scholars. In response to their criticism, Maxmuller has himself commented that, "We would not be able to lay down any terminus whether the Vedic hymns were composed in 1000 or 1500 or 3000 years B.C., no power on the earth could ever fix". According to Prof. Weber (c.f. *History of Indian Literature,* p. 4):

"Certainly, the most ancient literature (the Vedas) is available only in India".

MacDonell and Keith have approximated the period of Vedas as around 2000 to 1200 years B.C. Winternitz (pg. 6 of the Hindi translation of *Ancient Sanskrit Literature*) has inferred the time of Vedas to be around 2500 to 2000 years B.C. whereas Jacobi (in *Indian Antiquary*, Vol. 23, p. 158) takes it back to 4000 to 3000 years B.C. Thus, in all, the period of the Vedas is mostly approximated by the Western Scholars as 4000 to 1200 years B. C. It is anyway not possible for them to take the period of existence of anything before 4000 years B. C. because, as per the holy Bible, the age of present creation of the world is only around 6000 years; and the average time in which the above inferences were made by thinkers from Maxmuller to Jacobi was around 1950 AD.

Irrespective of their numerical estimates of the likely period of the Vedas, the Western scholars have all recognised the Vedas as the most ancient scriptures of knowledge for the human race (http://literature.awgp.org/akhandjyoti/2005/May_Jun/v1.VedicCosmology_3).

The Mahabharata alludes to the Vedas over and over again. That way we can assume the society of the Vedas and the tradition set down by the Vedas not only linger in the Mahabharata but also prevail in the Mahabharata in an elaborate way. So it will not be irrelevant to dwell on the context and the theme of the Vedas to trace the origin of the Mahabharata. According to the western scholars, the Vedas were composed by a race called the Aryans who migrated into India from somewhere beyond India, be it Central Asia or Germany. Once the notion of Aryan race is assumed and once it is assumed that the Aryans came from away, the whole gamut of ancient Indian literature beginning from the Vedas to the epic age could be interpreted in a particular way. Such assumptions seek to prove that the ancient literature in the mean is an allegory of the gradual conquest of the entire sub-continent of India by the so called race known as the Aryans. But in our opinion, this is farthest from truth. Firstly, the word Aryan has never been used in ancient literature as a race. The word Aryan could have many etymological interpretations. In our opinion it has been derived from verb Ri meaning to grow. And those people who were active and dynamic in the society were called the Aryans. They were the progressive among the masses. The western scholars posit that the Vedic hymns were written by a group of poets during the time when they were migrating into India from away. But people who are forced to migrate from their native land and who find fresh pastures in a new found land to settle are apt to hark back to their erstwhile home land just as the Christians hark back to Eden whence our first parents were thrown away. But a close reading of the Vedic hymns will not betray any longing lingering look back to any place beyond India which could be their home land. The hymns themselves allude to the five rivers of the Punjab as their goddesses or mothers. It takes a long time for one to look upon a strange shore as his or her motherland. And of course, the Vedas are the fountain head of the social system, economic system, political system and so on that we find in the Mahabharata.

It is clearly stated by VedaVyasa to his son Shuka that he prepared the Mahabharata from the ten thousand Rikhs or Mantras of the Rig Veda and the mysteries of all the Vedas were revealed in the book he compiled, with all the didactic stories and true accounts, in such a way as would teach them faith, instruction and wisdom (Chapter 245 of Shantiparva, verses 13 and 14). The Mahabharata as we have pointed out is a long narrative. It consists of eighteen parvas or sections. And the focus of our treatise will be the Shantiparva or the twelfth section.

A note on the context of the Shantiparva here will not be out of place. The Shantiparva opens presently after the Great War at Kurukshetra. The eleventh parva heard the mourns of thousands of women, mothers, wives, daughters and children at the hecatomb of Kurukshetra where countless soldiers and heroes did bite the dust in the great sacrificial fire called the Kurukshetra war. Yudhisthira, the eldest Pandava, who won the great battle, lamented about the mass killing of the near and dear ones. He wanted to renounce the world. He did not want to ascend the throne. It is interesting that it was not the one who lost the battle but the one who won the battle and gained the kingdom was in grief. In this dramatic situation a vast array of discourses showed up. His brothers, eminent sages, the creator of the Mahabharata the great Saint Veda Vyasa and the mentor of the Pandavas Lord Shri Krishna participated in the same.

The Shantiparva has three hundred and sixty five chapters. There are 13,716 number of shlokas or verses. It is divided into three sub books or parvas:

i. Raja Dharma Anushasana Parva. It consists of chapters: 1 to 130 & four thousand seven hundred and sixteen slokas or Verses. It describes the duties of a public authority king and his governance, the Varnashrama or caste system and its linkage with the economic activities, the righteous living norms and observance of Chaturashrama the four stages of living to attain liberation in details.

ii. Apad Dharma Anushaasana Parva consists of chapters 131 to 173 & one thousand six hundred and forty nine slokas. It describes the rules of conduct when one faces adversity.

iii. Moksha Dharma Parva consists of Chapters 174 to 365 & seven thousand three hundred and fifty one slokas. This Parva describes how one should follow the norms of righteous living to achieve moksha or emancipation or liberation.

Literature as such holds the mirror to a society. And no wonder that an epic of the Mahabharata size seems to hold out a mirror to the different aspects of the society and thoughts that were prevalent in India of the time in which it was composed. Since in absence of other evidences literature itself is a source of history, we hereby seek to decode economic thoughts and economic activity of the Mahabharata age. On the surface it seems that the compass of the Mahabharata is not restricted to the values and activity of a particular society. Because of the Ashwamedha Yajnas or during any royal festivity we find that kings and princes from countless places turn up. And think of Kurukshetra war where warriors from different countries assembled to fight either on behalf of the Pandavas or on the behalf of Kauravas. It has been something like a world war and greater in its intensity than the two world wars that the world has witnessed of late. The total number of men directly killed in the second Great War has been fifty to fifty six million (source Wikipedia)and the total number of Kshatriyas killed in the Kurukshetra war which lasted only for eighteen days was one billion, six hundred and sixty million and twenty thousand men. In the StriParva of the epic, Yudhisthira provided the above report on casualties to Dhritarashtra (Source Mahabharata, Book 11 (Stri Parva), Chapter 269 and 10).

This also shows that Mahabharata India was in touch with different states of the world. It goes without saying that such global war where different states of the world participate must have economic activities and network among them. The conflict between Pandavas and Kauravas was centred around some acres of land. One should not look upon this as a mere story come from the fantasy of a poet. India and Pakistan are at daggers drawn over a few acres of land in Kashmir. Earlier Russian army and Chinese army stood on the banks of Ussuri river over a border district.

And more to it there is evidence in the Vedas of maritime trade and adventures. The trade and commerce between two states is very much dependent on the political and sociological structure of the two states. The states that pin their faith on protectionism does not allow the import of luxury goods from foreign countries. And similar other instances could be multiplied. Hence economics of any particular society is dependent on the political substructure of the society. At the same time the political substructure of the society is dependent on the economic substructure of the society. Hence ours is a venture to explore the economic thought and activity and political thought and activity of the Mahabharata age that are commingled.

Any political thought and activity and economic thought and activity imply management. A state managed by a king will be different from a state run by a democracy. In the world today there are control economics and the free market economics. And no wonder that they depend on the different management principles. Thus, economic thought, political thought and management principles are inalienable from one another and they certainly are based on a world view. The Germany of Hitler pinned its faith on the Swastika and the superiority of the Aryans to other races. And it was Germany which invoked second Great War. Thus economics, political science, management principles and the world view go together. And hence from this perspective we are about to decode the Mahabharata society in this treatise.

In course of conversations among the best intellectuals of the Mahabharata society for clearing the doubts of Yudhisthira, multitude of motifs such as the duties of the Kshatriyas the warriors, the necessity of conflict with the ultimate objective of peace, need of a proper governance in a society and the necessity of proper distribution of king's wealth through *Yajna* showed up. And specially it was the patriarch of the Kuru clan Great

Bhisma who from his death bed of arrows gave his immense valuable set of advices and instructions on various treatises to Yudhisthira when Yudhisthira pondered over some crucial subjects needed to govern a state.

The Shantiparva is a genre of wisdom literature. There are stories and many of them were incidents of Pre Mahabharata society, narrated by Bhisma and other wise characters of the Mahabharata. The stories were mainly parables used to motivate Yudhisthira and to prepare him for the role of a competent public authority and to inculcate in him the importance of state and kingdom to be administered by the rule of Dharma.

The topic of peace can be studied from different perspectives. On the surface peace means absence of violence and dissension. However this is rather superficial. The real peace implies creativity on every level and tranquility. Creativity on the physical level and intellectual level goads man to what we call development in the economic sense of the term. A highly developed drainage system, numerous hamams, international style palaces do not mean development. They are catalysts to accelerate development which looks forward to the notion of brotherhood implanted in every heart. In the language of economics, peace is an optimum equilibrium situation or it could be called Pareto optimum situation. The present study of the Shantiparva is from the perspective of economic thoughts and the principles of management as discussed in the book of peace.

The ultimate objective of mankind is peace and the chapter is a study of how economic activities coupled with right management principles can give peace.

Methodology of the Present Study

The study of economic thoughts and principles of management in the Shantiparva of the Mahabharata impels us to adopt a new methodology. An interdisciplinary study of economics and literature needs a deep searching of economic ideas within literature and literature within economics. The Mahabharata, a genre of literature itself, depicted a society, the Mahabharata society. The present study views the Shantiparva as an alternative socio economic thought with its own ethics, culture, socio economic outlook, management principles and administrative norms that might apply in the world today with success. Thus consequently it is also a search for the epistemology of economics.

There are some recurrent motifs in the Shantiparva. the significant ones from the standpoint of the present study are decoding Vedic ideas of charity, the caste system Chaturvarna and its economic implications, the four phases of human life known as Chaturashram, symbolised as the code of righteous living, treasury and wealth in management, the significance of right time and distribution of surplus, Yajna, duties of a king, public finance, fiscal and monetary policies, public governance system, Dandaniti or justice, dharma or righteous living norms, rights, justice, prosperity and welfare of the people, and the subject of moksha or spiritual liberation through proper observance of righteous socio economic prescribed norms.

A frequency distribution table below gives an idea of some of the recurrent motifs:

Table 1 Frequency of Occurrence of Specific Words in the Text Shantiparva

Specific Words	Number of Occurrence
Wealth	219
Dharma	195
Yajna	103
Money	100
Desire	75
Punishment or Dandaniti	57
Tax	48
Peace	47
Sacrifice	39

Sceptre or Rod	37
Duties	37
Evil	35
Gold	34
Welfare	32
Business	30
Teacher	22
Cows	19
Ethics	19
Moksha or Liberation	19
Caste	16
Donation	16
Distribution	15
Offering	12
Consumption	11
Administration	10
Satisfaction	10
Production	9
Economics	7
Gift	6
Exchange	5
Student	4
Learning	3
Education	3
Demand	2
Economic System	2
Rajyalakshmi (the prosperity of a state)	2

(Source: Forged by the author herself)

A glimpse at the frequency distribution table, even without any deep reading of the chapter, gives an idea of the discourse. The concept of wealth, righteousness or dharma, money, Yajna the sacrifice rituals, punishment or Dandaniti, the use of sceptre to protect righteousness, desires, ethics, cow as wealth, gift, donations, taxes, peace are some notable themes of economics and management. Moreover the mention of the word teacher many times indicates the nature of the discourse. Frequency, however, does not necessarily assess the right weightage of a motif. There we might use Baysian statistics where belief has a function and even in frequency tables the reader reads his own mind because the reader cannot help it.

The study focuses on the issues thus relevant from the standpoint of economics. It is divided into the following chapters following this introductory one. The next chapter is a discussion on the Mahabharata itself and the Vedic literature. Any literature is itself a representation of the period in which it has been created or it can be said as a representation of a society in the piece of that literature be it a poem or prose itself. Thus any literature itself is a model for a study. Economic Thoughts in ancient India are found in the four Vedas (Bokare, p. 81). The vision of economic life in Vedic dharma is outlined by Dr. Radhakrishnan. It is an idealised economic life in Chaturvarga – dharma, artha, kama and moksha. He quotes Bhavabhuti, "Knowledge of philosophy is prized for attainment of truth, Wealth is desired only for the help it affords in the discharge of social, economic and religious duties, and obligations ..." (Radhakrishnan, 1948).

Bokare (Bokaro, p. 68) quotes the English translation of the Sanskrit stanza in Vedic literature:

> May all being be happy
> May all attain bliss
> May all see happy days
> May no one be subject to suffering

Bokare says that Hindu-economics for mankind is expressed in the above stanza in Vedic literature. Vyasdeva's vision in the above stanza and abundance of Vedic blessings are correlated. And the economic thoughts of ancient India is thus the economics of abundance, not the western concept of economics of scarcity. The Vedas and the Upanishads are sources for the theoretical framework of ancient Indian economics and the Shantiparva contains the guidelines to live a life in that way are described in various forms.

2

A Discussion on the Mahabharata and the Vedic Society

The word Veda means knowledge or wisdom. On the surface, Vedic society was pronouncedly a sylvan one. The composers of the hymns there lived in the clearings of the forests. Naturally the fruits and roots, milk and honey were the food for their subsistence in the main. And hence the western scholars surmised that the people who composed the Vedic hymns, their kins and hearers basically belonged to a rural life very close to nature. True that the Vedic hymns dwell on natural forces like wind and fire, rivers are a recurrent theme in them but one feels that the poet of season of mists and mellow fruitfulness ("Ode to Autumn", Keats) was not necessarily a farmer. Shelley of the "Ode to Westwind" did not live in the woodlands. Similarly it is rather too much of imagination when we surmise that the Vedic rishis belonged to forest only. They had no notion of the so-called development as descried in urban society. The hymns have been composed in a number of very sophisticated metres that speaks of their urbanity. Here we use urbane in the sense of sophistication. They did not surely belong to the primitive society. And Vedic hymns refer to a thousand pillared hall. Besides, sea voyages and trade are also alluded to. The western historians claim that the urban civilisation that was Indus valley civilisation belonged to an earlier age than the Vedic civilisation.

They named those who composed the Vedas as Aryans who migrated to India and it were they who might have pulled down the urban civilisation of the Indus valley decked with planned cities well laid out roads and drainage system, grand baths and so on. But this seems to be a myth with us created by the western people who set up colonies in India. It were the less civilised Romans who destroyed the Greek civilisation. It were the Barbarians and Huns who shattered the mighty edifice of Roman civilisation. Western people in the eighteenth, nineteenth and twentieth century set out for conquest of the rest of the globe in quest of gold. And of course everywhere they tried to destroy the civilisation if any. Think of the Maya civilisation. It was, as it were, they who killed the last person of the Maya civilisation. And so the Europeans read their own past in the ancient Indian history and created a myth. The myth could be summed up as follows: In the pre Vedic age there were indigenous people living in India. They were highly civilised and they set up what we call an Indus Valley civilisation. The people who have composed the Vedas migrated into India. It were they who destroyed the city civilisation of the indigenous people. They named the people of the Vedic culture as Aryans and the people who set up the Indus valley civilisation as non-Aryans. The Aryans came to India from abroad. And it is said that they destroyed the highly developed urban civilisation of the non-Aryans. But we say that it is all moon shine and myth. The Vedas are a vast literature. And nowhere we find any longing lingering look back to their lost homeland other than India. The poets of the Vedas address the five rivers of Punjab as their mother. And the people of the Vedas have not swooped upon any people in India the way Attila the Hun and the Barbarians, Vandals and Goths came upon the Romans. The demons in the Vedas must not be identified with any race living in India before the advent of the Vedic people. Take for instance Vritta the demon. What he did was to imprison the rivers and shut up their passage to fertilise the plains just as modern dams do. Vritta belonged to the same people who composed the Vedas. Indra killed the demon and released the rivers pent up in the caves. The world today also seems to lodge complaint with God, if any, in the heaven against the multinationals who have dammed and damned all the rivers and may be Indra might appear once gain to rescue the rivers and cows from their prison. So we might well argue that the Vedic people themselves participated during the Indus Valley civilisation. And if that we grant, trade with Mesopotamia and ancient India during the Vedic age is very much evident. But the composers of the Vedas were against the getting and spending of the urban culture. They were a band of Thoreaus (Thoreau the author of Walden) who left the cities to lead a life under the greenwood trees. And it seems that the Vedic people looked upon cow as wealth. It does not necessarily mean that when they undertook voyages across the seas in vessels they would carry cows to the strangers in exchange of other commodities. Just as any legal tender of a country is not acceptable in another country similarly cow was the medium of exchange in India but they might not function as money in other countries.

The Vedic civilisation has been the fountainhead of Indian civilisation of the epic age. The two great epics the Ramayana and the Mahabharata mentioned innumerable times about the Vedic rishis, the poet philosophers of the Vedic times and their teachings. Any study of the Indian epics needs a prior understanding of the Vedic thoughts.

The Vedas are the oldest scriptures and the earliest documents of the human knowledge. The four books of the Vedas are Rig, Sama, Yajur and Atharva. The Vedas in a nutshell consist of the hymns, ritualistic texts and guidelines on sacrificial duties. However, they are the repositories of spiritual knowledge embedded in all aspects of human life mostly the religious, social, economic and political ones.

Rig Veda, the earliest one is on philosophical thoughts and religion is a snapshot of the period. Though it is not meant an encyclopedia of social and economic conditions however, it gives an opportunity to have a glimpse on the socio economic thoughts of the ancient Vedic poet philosophers. For instance the Gambler's lament is a monologue of a repentant gambler in one hymn of the Rig Veda. He laments the ruin brought on him because of his addiction to the dice:

> The gambler's wife is left forlorn and wretched:
> The mother mourns the son who wonders homeless
> In constant fear, in debt and seeking riches,
> he goes by night unto the home of others.
> Sad is the gambler when he sees a matron,
> another's wife, and his sees a matron,
> Another's wife, and his well-ordered dwelling
> (Rigveda X, 34, 10-11)

The motif of ill effects of gambling in the cautionary poem of the Vedic poet repeats as one of the main themes of the epic literature Mahabharata. The game of dice ultimately causes the devastions in the Kurukshetra war. The hymn also throws light on the pattern of land ownership. It indicates that houses were owned in severalty and the owners had the right to transfer (Das, *The economic history of ancient India*, 1937). The villages were the basis of social life. The corporate character of the village life is mentioned in the hymns (Rigveda X).

Let linguists say whatever they can, the Vedas are the oldest extant work in any Indo European language. And hence if any Aryan race is assumed, its homeland must have been India. The earliest structure of Indian society and religion rests on the

Vedas. But the Veda was a sealed book to the common people both on account of its inaccessibility to the latter as well as its extreme condensation. As time wore on, from one Veda four Vedas grew, and their interpretations assumed the name of the fifth Veda, for the common people, as the Bharata Samhita, which afterwards developed into the great Indian epics, the Mahabharata and the Ramayana (Mullick). The Mahabharata is said to be fifth Veda (Mullick).

To give example of the elements of economics and how the Mahabharata society had been evolved from the Vedic society, we can refer to the Chaturvarna, Chaturashrama and the Chaturvarga. In order to full well understand the ancient Indian literature and economy we had better a close look at the caste system which largely constructed the structure of the society. In the Mahabharata the caste system was pronounced and it was the duty of all the governments, call them kings to preserve the caste system in the state. The highest voice in the Mahabharata viz. that of Lord Krishna who is God incarnate states that it is he who divided the society into four castes. Let us not waste our time here discussing whether the caste system is judicious or not. However the caste system could be traced back to the Pururshasukta of the Vedas.

The Purushasukta states that in the beginning when there was no time, no space, there was a being who had thousand heads and thousand eyes and thousand legs. Another being namely Virat sprang from him. And it was this Virat who first enacted sacrifice in the existence. It was Virat who sacrificed himself and it was through this sacrifice that the Brahmins leaped forth from his head and Kshatriyas sprang from his hands, the Vaisyas emerged from his thighs while the Surdas sprang from his legs. This clearly shows that the ancient Indian society was structurally raised on the station and duties of different people of a society. Those who were keen on metaphysical discourse were brahmins. They often lived far from the madding crowds ignoble strife to pursue spiritual quest and discourse. The Kshatriyas sprang from the hand of the Viratpurusha. They are fighters. They strive to protect the people from their wounds. So they are kings and princes and warriors. The Vaisyas sprang from the thigh of the Viratpurusha. They are actually travellers who create wealth by way of moving things from one place to another and adding wealth to the society. They are engaged in business activity. They are also farmers. Finally, there were shudras who sprang from the feet of the Virat Purusha. Thus with the sacrifice of the self of Viraat the four castes emerged. The shudras functioned as a support for the three other castes. In our opinion no caste in this context is superior or inferior to any other caste. There has been division of labour installed thereby but there was no hierarchy. During war times Kshatriyas should come to the fore. When trade and commerce is a fashion of the day, the Vaisyas should come to the force. And the Shudras were everywhere functioning as a support for every activity of every caste performing its duty. And ironically enough every Brahmin while sitting for his worship or pujas at the outset pays homage to the feet of Lord Vishnu who should be looked upon as the Virat purush. While Kshatriyas implement the law, there are Vaishyas who create wealth and produce food. And in every society there are people who serve the above classes or castes. But how can one put the right person at the right place? Confucius invoked meritocracy and introduced competitive exams. Confucius invented the notion that those who govern should do so because of merit, not of inherited status, setting in motion the creation of the imperial examinations and bureaucracies open only to those who passed tests" (Sienkewicz, 2003). In India the caste system was the answer. Krishna pointed out in the Gita that the four castes were forged on the basis of guna and karma. In fact, in those days, they judged the people on the basis of a priori aptitudes. Those who were apriori drawn to deliberation on metaphysical issues were brahmins and so on. May be the ancient people had a method to access the a priori aptitude of a child. Besides it seems that ancient India believed in the efficacy of heredity. So the caste system in ancient India seems to become hereditary. But it was not always that. A Brahmin was expected to follow knowledge like a sinking star. But maybe the son of a Brahmin could deviate from the path of spiritual studies. He could be deemed as a chandala.

The varied desires and occupations by different sections of the society, the economic interests intertwined with them and the creation of a social division because of it can be analysed from the following verse of the Rig Veda:

> Men's tastes and trades are multifarious,
> And so, their ends and aims are various.
> The smith seeks something cracked to mend,
> The leech would fain have sick to tend.
> The priest desires a devotee,
> From whom he may extract his fee.
> Each craftsman makes and vends his ware,
> And hopes the rich man's gold to share.
>
> (Rig Veda, IX, 112.1-2)

The Chaturashrama was the four age based and activity based life stages mentioned in details in the ancient Indian philosophical texts. The stages were Brahmacharya, Garhasthya, Vanaprastha and Sanyasa. In each stage of life in the context of Chaturashrama, the person is needed to perform his well-defined role and duties. The four stages of life consists of the stages of a student life, that of a householder, anchorite and finally that of a renouncer. It conveys the spirit of the Indian social order and demonstrates the concept of sacrifice and the yearning for liberation which is the core of Indian philosophy.

And Chaturashrama and the chaturvarga not only indicate the different stages of life, it also focuses on the quality of life a person should have. The Vedic philosopher poets expressed their reverence and love for Nature in their hymns. In the ancient Indian texts, especially in the epics, the role of Nature is of immense significance for both material pursuits as well as for spiritual liberation of a person. And to have a glimpse of the intimacy of man with Nature, a peep into the concept of Chaturashrama is important. In each and every stage, he is never separated from the Mother Nature.

The first stage of life was studentship in those days. A student left his home to stay in the house of the preceptor the Guru for many years and attained both spiritual and worldly knowledge. And the house of the Guru, the ancient *Gurukulas* the in-forest hermitages, was tucked away in the forests away from the sounds and shouts of mundane life. And the young students learned to make friends with Nature, respect its bountiful qualities and to take care of Nature's resources.

In the Shantiparva of the Mahabharata, the chapter on peace, there is detailed description of the specific duties of a householder which implies the second stage – the way of living of a householder. Among those duties the important commitments of a householder was to take care of the plants, to look after the birds and all the domestic animals. Moreover he was bound to provide sustenance to the sages who lived in the forests. A householder thus was aware of his duties for the other inhabitants of Nature and society. In fact the relationship between Nature and man is symbiotic. Nature gives man not only the fruits and the roots but it also maintains the environment. And just like a householder has responsibilities to his family and society, man has responsibility to Nature.

Just as man has responsibilities to his families, similarly the ruler, a public person has responsibility for good governance and public welfare. In this context, the protagonists of the Shantiparva, the political philosopher sages and especially the Patriarch Bhisma the repository of all administrative knowledge, referred to Nature as a great teacher. They explained to Yudhisthira the treatise of governance citing instances from Nature. Bhisma asked Yudhisthira to collect tax from his subjects just like a bee who collects honey from the flowers without injuring them.

In another instance, Vyasdeva advised Yudhisthira about the significance of the right time in any action. *Yudhisthira* was in deep anguish after the Kurukshetra war. Vyasdeva consoled him. He advised Yudhisthira to accept that the dead ones do not return. He explained that it is not possible to get anything until the right time comes. Only the right time can bring success and growth in any endeavour. Vyasdeva explicated how Nature is also tuned with the right time. Clouds bring rain when the time is right, trees do not bear any flowers and fruits untimely, animals do not have their sex untimely, all the seasons come at their right times, life begins and ends when time is due, children start to speak when the right time comes, adolescence comes in due time and plants begin to grow from seeds at the right time. The rising and setting of the sun, the waxing and the waning of the moon, the ebbs and flow of the sea all occur in right time.

Nature is also the source of livelihood. The forests were of great economic importance to the Mahabharata as well as to the earlier Vedic societies. They served as natural pastures. Cow rearing was the most significant activity in ancient India. And the forests provided the householder with the building materials for both home and transportation, fuel, sacrificial implements apart from food and specific medicines.

The third stage Vanaprastha in other words implies life in the forest. The phase was considered a transitional one. A person when approaching towards old age, his greater emphasis was expected to be on spiritual liberation or moksha instead of fulfilling material and physical pursuits of artha and kama. In the literal sense it means to be gradually detached from the worldly life and choose to retire to the forest. However, it may signify the beginning of return journey to Nature's lap. The mature person experienced with the joys and woes of the materialistic life during this stage could share his wisdom with the willing ones in the society to make the world a happier place to live in.

During the fourth stage or Sanyasa, the person became a wandering mendicant in the age of the Mahabharata, shunning all his attachments and possessiveness. And thus Nature was then the sole companion and the refuge for him. His focus would be on eternal peace.

The chaturashrama system of ancient India as deciphered from the Shantiparva of the Mahabharata thus guides the people to play the game of life. The mother earth is the stage where one struggles to achieve the supreme beatitude of life. It is the place of fulfilment of worldly duties and the preparation for the self realisation. And Nature herself nurtures through these four stages of life.

The study of these four stages of life in relation to Nature can be the basis of an alternative way of living. The modern approach of development economics focuses development as the enlargement of choices. And it is the quality of life which is considered to be of utmost importance. One can choose to be wealthy with minimum possession or material wealth. Wealth in real terms can be interpreted as the symbol of good life. And the world devastated day by day with loss of compassion for its green and the non-human species may learn from the Chaturashrama ideology how to be one with Nature.

Curiously enough the concept of Chaturashrama reminds one of the life cycle hypothesis as put forward by Franco Modigliani. Both focus on how should we participate in the creation of wealth and how should we use the wealth. Of course there is a difference between the two models because of the different perspectives from which the life is viewed.

An individual can realise him or herself by balancing and fulfilling these four objectives. They are not independent or mutually exclusive of each other and should not be viewed in a stand-alone manner. Exclusive pursuit of one Purushartha creates an imbalance in a person's life and prevents the person from reaching the ultimate destination of their life the self-realisation. Take Artha, for example. If an individual seeks only material wealth but lacks in righteousness, and the fulfillment of their duty, an emptiness and lack of self-liberation take hold.

The theme wealth has been a recurrent motif in the Shantiparva of Mahabharata. The third chapter is a study on wealth in the Shantiparva. The canvas of this book is immensely wide and wealth here is indeed a multi connotative term. However, one of the most valuable wealth was cow. The chapter also focuses on the treasury and wealth in management.

3

Cow – A Wealth in the Ancient Indian Literature and Archetypal in Present Indian Literature

Wealth is a subject which never becomes out of fashion for the thinking minds. And what is wealth is a million dollars question. What is wealth for one society may not be such for another. Moreover, what is cherished by our ancestors as wealth may not be such for us. This study is an attempt to find the deeper meaning of wealth in cow. And it looks beyond the traditional economic methodologies and searches the meaning of wealth through the literature of different eras. A piece of literature exposes the thoughts, aspirations, love and desires of the people of the period in which it is composed. It is their thoughts which create the wealth of a nation.

From the first section to the end, wealth is a keyword. In the beginning of Shantiparva, the post Kurukshetra war period, Yudhisthira was depressed. The great saint Narada wanted to know the reason why Yudhisthira had any grief after he owned wealth of the state. Narada mentioned the kingdom as Rajyalakshmi. It signifies that kingdom is itself as precious as the goddess of wealth or in other words the kingdom is the storehouse of wealth.

Moreover the concept of wealth was related to what was valuable at that time period. For instance, cows were considered as wealth. Cows were given to Brahmins as dakshinaa the voluntary payment after a Brahmin performed any ritual. Wealth has many functions to perform. But greed for wealth often leads to disaster.

Yudhisthira lamented that for greed of wealth and power, they had killed their own friends. He wanted to sacrifice all his material wealth and the desire for the same. Arjuna sought to change his elder brother's attitude towards material wealth.

Arjuna told Yudhisthira, that Yudhisthira was born in a king's family. After the win he became the master of the whole world. His duty was to organise Yajna, the sacrificial ceremony for distribution of wealth. Thus from Arjuna's conversation the role of a king or an administrator becomes clear. Arjuna's argument for the need of wealth was very significant. The wealth was considered from different aspects, from the role of king or any public administrator to a common person.

Arjuna first alerted his brother who would be king soon, the need of proper distribution of wealth. A king or a public administrator, first of all, should look upon his subjects. The duty of an able administrator is the proper distribution of wealth for a just society. A proper distribution of wealth is an essential precondition for any economy be it a monarchial one or a democratic one.

Arjuna explained that the dharma of the kings is observed with the provision of wealth. It is interesting to note that Arjuna stressed on the issue of dharma of the king. The word dharma itself has more than one connotation. It signifies morale, it signifies the roles and duties of the authority of public exchequers.

The analysis of wealth in the discipline of economics today has walked a long path. After the end of the Cold War, Marxism subsided, capitalism became supreme, and now the overwhelming teaching in economic theory has become some branch of neoliberal theory. Neoliberal economic theory – game theory, econometrics, cost-benefit analysis – based around the concept of an economic agent whose moral compass is self-interested optimal utility. In theory, if the self-interest of each agent is left to its own devices, this will maximize the benefit of the whole.

An issue today is that many believe the benefit of the whole does not seem to be the case, as economic theory predicts. There continues to be greater wealth inequality and concentration, rampant unemployment, overpopulation, climate change, environmental degradation, among other issues.

The conversation of Arjuna and Yudhisthira in the Shantiparva showed that the economic agent was fully enveloped by evolving political philosophy and its moral code.

In this context, the view of the western philosophers regarding the subject of political economy can be looked upon. Xenophon's term Oeconomicus, one of the earliest works coining a definition of economics, is regarding man and his management of the household. Xenophon's writing introduces a concept of economic man whereas Plato's *Republic* seems to become much more influential in the course of economic theory and its history. In the *Republic* Plato introduces a concept of a political economy where individuals are parts of a grand hierarchical order that can move towards a Platonic "ideal" society if each individual performs their "true" function. The philosopher-kings, the carpenters, the soldiers, the slaves have a place that can align with this Platonic enlightened society.

Plato's concept of a political economy is similar to the father of modern economics, Adam Smith's, idea of the "invisible hand".

Smith believed that if each economic agent acted through self-interest it would be as if an "invisible hand" guiding the society in the optimal direction. Society, to Plato, moves towards the "ideal" – the true, the good, and the beautiful – political order if each individual following a priori aptitude his innate role, whether it is to be a soldier, a philosopher-king, a slave, and so on. Plato's "ideal" becomes Smith's "invisible hand."

After the Greeks, Thomas Hobbes became influential in the discipline of economics by introducing his concept of the social contract and man's innate self-interest. His work *Leviathan* establishes the idea that individuals are suspicious and self-interested in the most primitive aspects of our being. Our "state of nature" according to Hobbes is a place that is "nasty, brutish, and short" because we are essentially killing each other off out of suspicion and constant threat. Anarchy is a terrifying state to Hobbes. To curb our most primitive instincts we establish a social contract (*i.e.* government) to establish rules, order and regulation, so we can live in a society that is much better than our primitive chaotic "state of nature." The social contract, *i.e.* Leviathan/ government, is a bit like the "invisible hand" in that it effectively becomes a third person guiding society – each individual collects and creates the "third person" as a whole.

Adam Smith came shortly after Hobbes. Smith appears to have contradictory views on how human beings relate to each other. In a *The Theory of Moral Sentiments* he expresses the view that human beings are ultimately sympathetic towards each other. In *The Wealth of Nations* he seems to say that have selfish motives. The ambiguity of Smith's ethics weakens his potential influence on the role of morals in modern day economics. As

Hobbes's view on self-interest was already more dominant Smith's self-interest perspective was emphasized while his sympathetic perspective waned.

Hobbesian social contract and Leviathan, as with Plato's "ideal" Republic, and Smith's "invisible hand," cannot be merely viewed from the perspective of the individual unit. There is a "third" person, a grand other that is persistently present as the higher moral order that guides the society. Thus, because economic theory's analytics is based on individual self-interest, it is blinkered. The problem is that the theory does not understand the greater whole to which each individual unit relates. The relationship between the individual and the greater whole has moral implications.

The Shantiparva of the Mahabharata prompt us to rediscover this moral dimension that needs to be integrated into, and not dismissed from contemporary economic theory.

For instance, Cow is the most important economic wealth in ancient India. What is wealth? Kautilya's *Arthashastra,* the masterpiece on statecraft, written at least one thousand five hundred years ago, declares that the source of livelihood is wealth. Among the sources of livelihood described there, cows played significant roles.

Not only the *Arthashastra*, since the days of the Vedas, the whole gamut of literature especially the epics the Ramayana and the Mahabharata are loud with the praise of cow.

The ancient Indian philosophers, the Vedic rishis and their progenies were conscious not only of the human inhabitants of the mother earth but also of all the living creatures and the environment. They advised people to learn the way of living by observing the way of living of other creatures, especially the cows in many contexts. No doubt with this unclouded insight, they could declare: 'Just as the cows love their calves, you too love each other'. Let us go through the evaluation of cow in ancient Indian literature.

Cow in Vedic Literature

The earliest stage of civilisation is taken to be the hunting stage. As the hunting age passes to the pastoral and animals are domesticated, the animal itself, not its skin, becomes the unit of value. The most common of such animals in India is the cow which is mentioned in the Rigveda. There is a hymn in this Veda where Indra is offered as a fetish for ten cows and another where Indra is considered to be so invaluable that not a hundred, a thousand or a myriad of cows can replace it.

The sutras of Panini have a large number of words which prove the existence of barter in his time. From Panini, we find that *gopuchchha* or bovine tail also acted as a medium of exchange. A more common standard of value was, however, the cow. In illustration of Panini sutra "Taddhitarthottara-pada-samahareca" we have the word *pancagu* which means anything bought in exchange for five cows. Similarly in the *Dharmasutras* we find that all fines for murder are reckoned in cows.

Cow Economy in the Arthashastra

The *Arthashastra* mentions that cattle rearing is the second most important economic activity after agriculture (1.4.1). They are the main source of wealth. The king obtains through them the treasury and the army, which brings under control both his own people and the enemy's people. Cows and she-buffaloes are reared for milk and the bulls and he – buffaloes are used as draught animals (2.29.41, 42). Ghee or the clarified butter which has the advantage of being easily stored and transported, is the main end product. Cheese is supplied to the army. Buttermilk is fed to dogs and pigs and whey mixed with oil cake is used as animal feed. There are scheduled lands for pasture. Cowherds are considered important because of the variety of benefits they provide. They also made agriculture and other activities possible by opening up pasture lands.

Private owners of animals pay a sales tax for every animal sold. All livestock owners are obliged to pay a special levy in times of financial stringency. Cows provide major source of revenue for the government.

The *Arthashastr*a has also elaborate evidence of Kautilya's concern for the protection of the cows. Village headmen are responsible for preventing cruelty to animals. Stray cattle are to be driven off with a rope or a whip without harming them. (3.10.30-34). Riding or driving a temple animal, a stud bull or a pregnant cow is prohibited (4.13.20). The possibility of herdsmen starving calves of their mother's milk is foreseen, milking cows twice in seasons when they should be milked only once is punished by cutting off the thumb of the culprit, killing or inducing someone to kill animals in cow herds are punishable by death (2.29.3,16.32). Special provisions are made for looking after nonproductive cattle (2.29.6).

Cow – A Recurrent Motif in the Shantiparva of The Mahabahrata

The cow is a recurrent motif in the Mahabharata. The society depicted in the Mahabharata is agrarian. Cattle and land are the major components of wealth in a kingdom. Cattle theft is a common theme in the Mahabharata. Moreover, references to pastoral lands being included in forest areas and cattle expeditions for counting cows and branding calves are included in the Mahabharata.

The name of the cow is mentioned at least thirty times in different contexts in the Shantiparva. Shantiparva tells us why Karna the great hero of the Mahabharata had his chariot stuck into the earth during his battle with Arjuna which became the swan song of his career. It is said that he had killed a cow earlier in his life. Karna wanted to make amends of his sin by offering cows to the owner of the dead cow. But that cannot work because every animal has the right to live on this earth. No compensation can make amends of killing a living person be it man or an animal.

Cow in the Mahabharata is an indicator of good governance. Devarshi Narada in the Shantiparva, narrates to Yudhisthira, the story of Rama the son of king Dasaratha. Ramrajya stands out in Indian mythology as an ideal instance of good government.

To prove the prosperity of Ramrajya, Narada observes that every cow during the reign of Rama used to give a pitcher full of milk every day. In other words when there is good government the environment becomes such that nature including plants and animals seem to bless us with plenty. And surely cow was the wealth in the then society of the Ramayana and the Mahabharata because it was the major source of livelihood for many.

The cow is given as an honorarium to the teacher and the priest. It was a principal wedding gift in the world of the Mahabharata. The ancient Indian economic system was focused mainly on charity and reciprocity. Reciprocity and gift economy are based on long term social relationship not a one-to-one give and take relationship between the two individuals. The charity practiced during the Yajnas is an instance of reciprocity.

There are multiple instances of donation of cows to the Brahmins or the teacher class of the society in the Shantiparva. The Brahmins were the most respected ones in the Mahabharata society though they were not economically the most powerful ones.

They were the teachers, the priests and the advisors regarding both the material and spiritual pursuits. And their sustenance was the responsibility of the society. And cow was the primary source of sustenance for the Brahmins. May be the Brahmins as a caste are no longer that honourable. But the priests and the scholars and the teachers are very much there. Do we not think that it is the duty of the society to serve them whatever they need?

Shantiparva of the Mahabharata is a discourse on an ideal state. Shantiparva itself belongs to remote past. And curiously enough Shantiparva which belongs to remote past dwells on the remote past in relation to the composition of Shantiparva itself. And there numerous episodes have been recounted as to how the eminent personalities of yore carried out the four pursuits of life where gifts or giving away of wealth was a must. They did not reject material wealth, but they knew its worth and distributed wealth judiciously among the deserving ones. Cow was a favourite for donation and dakshina or honorarium in the Mahabharata as well as in the pre Mahabharata society.

Cow was considered so valuable in the Mahabharata that it has been said that a forest could be burnt to protect a cow. It does not necessarily mean that the forests were looked upon as trifle. More instances could be cited from the Mahabharata as to the cow as a value. And the utility of the cow has developed into love and reverence for it as a chip in the hardware of Indian national mind. This has been evident from modern Indian literature as well. And the love for cow is archetypal in Indian literature today. K. V. Dominic an Indian English poet of today proves our point.

K.V. Dominic's 'A Cow on the Lane'

K. V. Dominic is an Indian English poet of eminence. Let us read a poem by him entitled "A Cow on the Lane" (Dominic, K. V. 2011). The poem starts with the hurly burly of modern time. The train would leave after fifteen minutes and the poet needs to drive five more miles to catch it. And a cow lies on the lane. In response of honking, she did not move. The poet felt that the cow retorted not to disturb her. Her posture reminded the poet of the Mahabharata and the Ramayana at that crucial time. Once, Bhimasena the Pandava famous for his strong physique was on his way to bring a special flower for their precious common better half Draupadi. Surely it was a very special task. And he saw a monkey blocking the road. And when Bhimasena with his arrogance ordered him to leave the path, the monkey just requested him to lift his tail and go. And Bhimasema failed to lift it. The monkey was Hanumana one of the finest characters of the Ramayana who was also the elder brother of Bhimasena from the father's side. Hanumana taught his arrogant brother to abandon his ego and insolence. The ancient philosopher poet Vyasa intertwined the two great epics and the Indian philosopher poet of today learned to be egoless and humane from the story. With folded hands he humbly requested the cow to clear the road. And as if the cow spoke through the poet's subconscious mind that there are many roads and the world is vast and wide. The world is not one's private property. And the poet listened to what his subconscious mind in the form of cow advised. He moved backwards, took another path and reached the station just on time.

Cow here is the motif which connects the thoughts of the modern Indian philosopher poet Dominic to the ancient Indian core philosophy. K. V. Dominic is an Indian English poet who has never been outside the arena of the epics the Mahabharata and the Ramayana. There are more than one interpretations of this poem. Of course, in spiritual sense, there are many ways to achieve peace – the destination. However, one should be free of his ego and be aware of the desires of the others. And in worldly sense, the present advanced capitalist economic system is based on aggression and market capture. And all the powerful players in this system treat the earth as their private property. The option of live and let live is not their criterion. However, it is a very myopic approach. The war-torn world is now concerned with how to achieve peace. And Dominic's poem "A Cow on the Lane' is surely a pathfinder in the pool of good thoughts of the people who are in search of peace. K. V. Dominic's "A Cow on the Lane" indeed substantiates the truth that the love for cow is archetypal in Indian literature today.

Wealth is dynamic. It needs attention. And here comes the discussion on treasury and the role of state in the Shantiparva.

Treasury and Wealth in Management – The Economic Thoughts in The Shantiparva of The Mahabharata

The strength of a government is its treasury. In any form of government, be it a monarchial one or a democratic one, treasury needs a vigilant eye all the time. Treasury, be it the funds or revenue of a state, institution or society or be it a collection of valuables or delightful things is a subject of priority to whoever is in charge of it.

The longest epic of the world, the Mahabharata, has pondered over this subject time and again. The magnitude and grandeur of the Mahabharata's philosophical depth can be summarised in one of its quotes which states that what is not found here, will not be found elsewhere. The main story revolves around two branches of a family – the Pandava and Kauravas. In the Kurukshetra War, they battle for the throne of Hastinapura.

Among the major causes of the great war of Kurukshetra, the immense valuables of the kingdom of Hastinapura as well as that of the kingdom of Indraprastha certainly had their subtle role in influencing the bloodbath.

The greatest intellectual minds of the Mahabharata society spoke their minds on treasury, how to preserve it, how to augment it and many other issues connected with it in great details. Though some of them were having been true for the Mahabharata society and monarchical structure, but, many of those thoughts are universal and have relevance in the present scenario. It needs no clarification that treasury in some form or other was a priority then and it is a priority now for any government for the administration as well as welfare criteria.

The great Patriarch of the Kaurava clan Bhisma gave advice to Yudhisthira in the Shantiparva, the chapter on peace. Yudhisthira obeying the advice of Lord Krishna requested the knowledgable Bhisma about the duties of a king and the management of the state. Bhisma stated that without the four principles of human object Dharma the righteousness, Artha the material wealth, Kama the passion and Moksha the spiritual wisdom, the purpose of a king cannot be accomplished only with what is lotted. He advised Yudhisthira that he should always endeavour to obtain the four principles of human object. Administration followed by Dharma is the main duty of a king. But Dharma, cannot be achieved without artha as Bhisma opined in the context of administration of the state. He narrated the importance of the kingdom and material wealth to Yudhishthira, who was indifferent towards the kingdom.

The discourse also throws light on the ethics of an administrative authority, be it a dynastic king or an elected government. The pre requisite of any strong government for the welfare of his subjects is a sound treasury. And the first criterion for that is to collect wealth. Here Shantiparva has some advices. Many of them may not be go well together with the conventional idea of ethics, peace and cooperation.

Bhisma advised that a king should acquire wealth from his own state or from other states. It is because treasury is the fulcrum for righteousnes and expansion of a kingdom. The Sanatana Dharma or the Universal Righteous duty according to Bhisma is acquisition of wealth, its careful protection and the augmentation of that wealth and property. He did not recommend any extreme to do that. A ruler should not acquire wealth only by cruelty or only by honesty. A combination of civility and cruelty is necessary for the collection of wealth for the treasury.

The protagonist in the Shantiparva has clarified the reasons for using harsh means in details. A weak ruler cannot acquire wealth, and, the wealthless person is a weak one. A weak ruler cannot rule for long. He loses his dignity after he loses his crown. And for a public figure, losing dignity is like his own death. A ruler thus has needs to adopt the strategy to expand his wealth, strength and number of friends. Wealth, strength and friends have positive correlations. Nobody wants to be a friend to a poor and weak person.

Moreover, the common people disregards a ruler who is weak because he cannot satisfy their aspiration of being rich. A poor head of the state means the economy is in miserable state and the citizens also remain in poverty. Consequently they lack the vigour to do any work for the sake of the head of the state. Any head of a state is considered a powerful one and is respected one only because of his wealth. The Shantiparva draws an illustration that like clothes which covers private parts of a body of a woman, wealth and property of a king covers all his sins (Mahabharata, Shantiparva, Ch. 133, Canto 1-7).

Be that as it may, no one can doubt that a rich country is a powerful one and can dictate what is moral and immoral in a particular time and space. For example, USA imposes different rules regarding pollution on developing nations. If they make the first move in attacking a less developed country they justify it by saying that the attack is in need of the hour for greater peace and so on.

The protagonist Bhisma in the Shantiparva has defined wealth as valuable or worthless according to its right use. Who do not respectfully feed the gods, forefathers and the people, their wealth are considered as valueless. And that wealth should be confiscated by an honest head of the state and should be distributed among the needy deserving people. The authority should not hoard that wealth to augment the treasury. A *Dharmajna* or a righteous person is one who knows how to earn, how to get hold of wealth of dishonest persons and to distribute them to the honest ones. (Shantiparva, Chapter 136, Canto 5-7)

It is noteworthy that dharma and artha are not considered opposed to each other. A person is known as a knowledgeable one if he knows how to collect wealth from the dishonest persons who do not follow the norms of the society and to give the wealth to the righteous ones. Moreover, loss of revenue of the state authority leads to the loss of strength of the latter. It is advised therefore that the kings should always carefully protect the treasury because it is the treasury which is the main strength of the king. (Shantiparva, Ch 119, Canto 16). And a king needs to preserve his treasury as earnestly as we save water in a desert region. (Shantiparva, Ch-130, Canto-12-13).

When a king uses coercive policy or force for revenue collection it ultimately brings disaster for the king. The combined grief of the unhappy citizens leads to the destruction of king's life, strength and his treasury. Think the fate of Louis XVI. The common people thus should not be treated thoughtlessly. The honest citizens are strong ones (Shantiparva, Ch. 130, Canto 9). This advice is a timeless one. Any coercive means of revenue collection can be fatal for the government.

However, if any emergency arises for the state, and, if the citizens are not eager to donate money to the king's exchequer, the king can be a dictator one, take their wealth as the wealth belonging to the state and keep the treasury in his personal control. (Shantiparva, Ch. 87, Canto 23-24). One can find the applicability of this policy in the present time period as well. For instance, they say that the amount of black money has been so huge that it seemed to strangle the market. Hence, all of a sudden, the citizens of India experienced the impact of a demonetisation policy declared by the democratically elected Government of India in the November 2016 citing the need of emergent problem of amassing of huge black money in the Indian economy.

The centre of power of a king is his treasury and his soldiers. Without a well maintained treasury, it is not possible to maintain a strong military force. Soldiers are needed for protection of the *Dharma* the righteousness. And righteousness is the support base for the citizens. Therefore, the treasury which is the foundation of all of them should be augmented. (Shantiparva Ch 130, canto 35). The war ravaged world today seeks peace. A large part of planned budget every year for most of the countries is for military purpose. the justifications for military expenses by any one, be it the speaker the stalwart Bhisma of the Mahabharata society or be it any statesman of today, rather sound similar that all are for protecting the people's right. However, peace seems to be as unsustainable as sustainable development.

There are more justifications in Shantiparva for state administered oppression to the people in the need of state. Bhisma admitted that collection of revenue for the treasury cannot be achieved without oppression. And without money, armed forces cannot be maintained. Therefore, a king must not be blamed if he oppresses people for revenue collection. (Shantiparva, Chapter130, Canto 36) It is further stated that the people who oppose the motive of enriching the treasury have to be killed to fulfill the objective of revenue optimisation. (Shantiparva, Chapter 130, Canto 42) The ethics of the head of the state is therefore different from the ethics of the common man.

There are justifications for having wealth. Wealth helps one to enjoy both present life and life after death. If one has wealth, he can spend it for praiseworthy righteous activity and can be able to attain a higher spiritual phase after death. The Mahabharata believes that the soul is deathless and one faces consequence for all his or her great deeds and wrongdoings after the death of the physical body. A poor person cannot observe dharma or maintain truth and lead a death in life (Shantiparva, Chapter 130, Canto 43) Does this signify that the means justify the ends?

Be that as it may, it is also well known that the great sages of ancient India were not respected for their material wealth but for their intellectual and spiritual wealth. And the people from all spheres of life including the kings and the rich people of the society used to meet them for advice both for worldly matters as well as for intellectual pursuits.

There are noteworthy observations regarding personal wealth in the Shantiparva. It is noted that the acquisition of wealth and sacrifice of wealth cannot be done in one generation. No one can find a rich old man in a forest. People always desire to grab whatever wealth in the world they find. (Shantiparva, Chapter 130, Canto 45-46)

People earn and save wealth with their intelligence and skill as Bhisma explained to Yudhisthira. The wise persons call the poor persons the weak ones and the rich persons as the strong ones. Nothing is beyond reach for a rich person and a king with a praiseworthy treasury wins over all dangers. All the righteous duties, fulfillment of passion, happiness in present life and that after death is achieved with a well maintained coffer, because a rich state can revel in the welfare activities for its people. Bhisma advised to Yudhisthira that he should desire to achieve that wealth through righteous means and never be tempted to attain wealth through wrongful means. (Shantiparva, Chapter 130 Canto 48-50). However it has been discussed earlier that an apparently oppressive policy is considered a right one for the sake of the security of the state and the kingdom. Thus right or wrong is context based.

A considerable discourse on the subject of wealth, treasury and how to attain wealth in the Shantiparva of the Mahabharata is itself a treasure in the pool of ancient Indian economic thoughts whose basis is spirituality. Wealth is a vehicle to live two hundred percent, one hundred percent materially and one hundred percent spiritually. And with subtle reasoning, the great Patriarch explained that why and how the material wealth and the treasury dictate the righteousness, the Dharma and satisfy the passion or Kama.

The subject of wealth brings in front some significant issues which are relevant from the standpoint of economics and management. The next chapters are analysis of Raj Dharma, the necessity of a ruler, the duties and functions of the king or the state administration.

4

The Necessity of a Ruler: The Socio-Economic Perspectives of the Shantiparva in the Mahabharata

Why did the necessity of a government or a ruler emerge in the lives of the people? Yudhisthira wanted to know this from his great grandfather Bhisma in the Shantiparva of the Mahabharata. Bhisma, the patriarch of the Kuru dynasty was lying on the death bed of arrows. Yudhisthira agreed to become the king after being counseled by the philosopher sages. Advised by Lord Krishna, he went to Bhisma. Lord Krishna, the friend and guide of the Pandavas was all praise for Bhisma. He acknowledged Bhisma as a great man who knows the past, present and the future and lamented that after Bhisma's death, the world would be as dark as that of a moonless night. He advised Yudhisthira to meet him at the earliest and know from him about everything of the state administration.

State – The View of the Political Thinkers

The state and the necessity of the head of a state – a central power are the subject of discussion among the political philosophers for centuries. The state is constituted by the combination of all the inhabitants in a certain area using their united force in accordance with the commands of a Government. Both, the ancient Indian philosophers and political thinkers as well as that of the western philosophers dwell on the various functions of state like governance, administration, defence, law and order. The *Arthashastra* written by Chanakya, the 4th century BC Indian political philosopher, provides an account of the science of politics for foreign affairs and wars, the economic stability of the state and many other topics of state administration. Chanakya quotes several authorities including Brihaspati, Prachetasa Manu and Parasara. Sukracharyya Neeti is also an influential extant Indian treatise on political philosophy. The Laws of Manu or Manusmriti as well as Sukra Neeti refer to the code of law in ancient India.

During the European Renaissance, Niccolo Machiavelli's The Prince written between 1511-12 presents a pragmatic view of politics, where, good and evil are mere means used to bring about a secure and powerful state. At the start of the 17th century Thomas Hobbes, the proponent of the theory of social contract goes on to expand this view. Both Machiavelli and Hobbes believed in the inherent selfishness of the individual. It was necessarily this belief that led them to adopt a strong central power as the only means of preventing the disintegration of the social order.

The Ram Rajya in the Ramayana

The great Indian epics, the Ramayana and the Mahabharata dwell elaborately on the necessity of an efficient king, the ideal state and governance. Ram Rajya, the kingdom of Shri Rama is referred to as a model one even today when one speaks what is meant by a peaceful state. Ram Rajya in the Ramayana society is referred to as an ideal society where everybody follows a code of righteous living and everybody is more or less happy, getting all their essential needs. Ram Rajya, the kingdom of Shri Rama is referred to as a model state by none other than Mahatma Gandhi (cp Hind Swaraj).

Shantiparva – The necessity of 'Raajan'

In the Shantiparva of the Mahabharata, Bhisma, the protagonist, lying on the bed of arrows, narrated the importance of kingdom to Yudhisthira, who was earlier indifferent to the necessity of a king. Yudhisthira asked Bhisma about the etymology of the word 'Raajan' or king and asked about the evolution of the notion of Raajan. Bhisma explained that at the very outset of the Satyayuga, there was neither a kingdom, nor a king, neither any punishment nor an authority to give the order to punish. All the inhabitants looked after each other obeying the dharma which means observation of their right roles and duties. However, after some time period, delusion began to grasp them. They lost consciousness as the do's and dont's. People became greedy. They got trapped into unreasonable desires and lust. Consequently, they became slave to the attachments. And the situation demanded the necessity of a Raajan – a king.

Thus Bhisma believes in a stateless society. This reminds us of the state of Nature as depicted by Rousseau. According to Rousseau, during the state of Nature there were paradise upon earth. Everybody would get whatever she or he needed. But Proudhon asserted that private property was theft. And Rousseau observed that with the advent of the private property, men started fighting among themselves impelled by greed. Life became unbearable. At that time everyone used to rule himself. But now the members of the society delegated each one's right to rule himself to the General Will. Be that as it may, the political thoughts like Marxism or Anarchism look forward to a stateless society as the ideal to be achieved by the civilisation.

Serene will be our days and bright,

And happy will our nature be,
When love is an unerring light,
And joy its own security.
And they a blissful course may hold
Even now, who, not unwisely bold,
Live in the spirit of this creed;
Yet seek thy firm support, according to their need.
("Ode to Duty", William Wordsworth)

In fact Satyayuga upholds anarchism. But lack of imagination and greed decreed the fall of man from the Eden of abundance and abandon. And that is the state of the society that we must look forward to. But it is a pity that greed and selfishness stand in the way. No political revolution, no materialistic revolution, no legislation can deliver us the goods. What is imperative is to revolutionise human character and behaviour. And the goals led down by the Mahabharata exhorting us to pursue the Chaturvarga –dharma, artha, kama, moksha can alone invoke the ideal society – a paradise upon earth. As long as the characters and behaviours of the people are not streamlined, Bhisma posits in the Mahabharata that there should be the necessity of a state and its ruler. In fact the king or the government must dispel the tama guna that clouds our consciousness with greed. The king or the Raajan is the emblem of Rajas that fights out the prevalence of Tama. This leads us to the deliberation of the three gunas.

The Raja Guna – Drive for Economic Activities

Here we had better digress into how nature and human nature are explored and explicated by ancient India. The approach of modern science is basically quantitative. If two bell jars of hydrogen and one bell jar of oxygen are mingled, there is water. But science cannot tell us how the waterness of water with its liquidity and thirst quenching power is derived from the oxygen ness of oxygen and hydrogen ness of hydrogen. Hence the proposition – hydrogen and oxygen make water is not truth or the probability of getting water through mingling hydrogen and oxygen could be 0.999...infinity. It is never one. And curiously enough this quantitative approach cannot throw any light on human character. The proper study of mankind is man. If man cannot be studied through any discipline be it economics or political science or physiology, then all the efforts of study come to naught. On the other hand Indian approach to the world and man is qualitative. There are three qualities in Sattva, Rajas and Tamas. While Sattva is light and while it is open and above board, tamas is heavy and dark. Tamas strives to hide everything. Between these two poles, Rajas moves to and fro.

In this context we can surmise that the majority of the people of a state goaded by greed and corruption remains underdeveloped. It is the Rajas the Raja or the rulers who must charge the idle folk with vitality and economic activity with a view to pursuing dharma, artha, kama, moksha.

All the worldly activities including economic, political and social ones fall in the domain of Rajasic Guna. The fourteenth chapter of the Bhagavad Gita concerns itself with the three modes of material nature – Gunatraya. Guna is chord or strand. The nature or Prakriti is like a rope made of three cords or gunas plaited together. As one of the constituent features of Nature, Guna denotes a quality or attribute of Prakriti, a way of manner in which it acts... Nature moves in repeating cycles of creation, maintenance and destruction and re-creation. Implications of these qualities are manifested in the nature in its different forms. As Lord Krishna explained his beloved friend and follower Arjuna that Sattva attaches to happiness, Rajas to action and Tamas attaches to miscomprehension. And a government, be it a monarchy, aristocracy or democracy, no doubt, fall in the domain of Rajas. Rajas is attached with power. Any authority seems to hold some power can create or destroy the tamas qualities among the people who are administered.

An Able Ruler Ushers in an Era

Bhisma, an authority in the subjects of politics and administration explained to Yudhisthira, the nitty gritty of the role of a king. According to Bhisma, Righteous administration is the main duty of a king and when a king properly uses the policy of punishment, once again Satyayuga begins on this earth. The king has been instrumental in the creation of Krta, Treta, Dvapara and Kali Yugas. This involves a philosophy in history. Yuga in the ancient Indian philosophy is an epoch or era within a four-age cycle. A complete Yuga starts with the Satya Yuga, via Treta Yuga and Dvapara Yuga and is clinched up with Kali Yuga. Our present time is considered to be a Kali Yuga, which started at 3102 BCE with the end of the Kurukshetra War or the Mahabharata war. Satya Yuga also known as Krita Yuga was the first and best Yuga, the age of truth and perfection. Humans were gigantic, powerfully built, honest, youthful, vigorous, erudite and virtuous. There was no agriculture or mining as the earth yielded those riches on its own. Weather was pleasant and everyone was happy. There were no religious sects. There was no disease, decrepitude or fear of anything.

When love is an unerring light and joy its own security, the society needs no positive law and a government. This puts in our mind Shakespeare in *The Tempest.*

In *The Tempest*, Gonzalo observes:

> I'th commonwealth I would by contraries
> Execute all things, for no kind of traffic
> Would I admit; no name of magistrate;
> Letters should not be known; riches, poverty,
> And use of service, none; contract, succession,

> Bourn, bound of land, tilth, vineyard, none;
> No use of metal, corn, or wine, or oil;
> No occupation; all men idle, all,
> And women too, but innocent and pure;
> No sovereignty –
> ....
> All things in common nature should produce
> Without sweat or endeavor; treason, felony,
> Sword, pike, knife, gun, or need of any engine,
> Would I not have; but nature should bring forth
> Of its own kind, all foison, all abundance,
> To feed my innocent people.
>
> *(Shakespeare, The Tempest 2.1.162-171; 175-180)*

Treta Yuga is considered to be the second Yuga in order, virtue diminishes slightly. At the beginning of the age, many emperors rose to eminence and conquered the world. Wars became frequent and the weather began to change to extremities. Oceans and deserts were formed. People became slightly diminished compared to their predecessors. Agriculture, labour and mining became existent.

Dvapara Yuga is considered to be the third Yuga in order. In this age, people became tainted with evil qualities and were not as strong as their ancestors. Diseases became rampant. Humans were discontented and fought each other. People still possessed characteristics of youth in old age. Average lifespan of humans was around a few centuries.

Kali Yuga is the final age. It is the age of darkness and ignorance. People become sinners and lack virtue. They become slaves to their passions and are no match for their earliest ancestors in the Satya Yuga. Society falls into disuse and people become liars and hypocrites. Knowledge is lost and scriptures are devalued. The environment is polluted, water and food become scarce. Wealth is heavily diminished. Families become non-existent. By the end of Kali Yuga the average lifespan of humans will be short.

There are forty one cantos in the Shantiparva which dwell specifically on the necessity of an able administrative head, the king, in the society of the Mahabharata. The cantos were classified below into different headings according to their socio economic ideas.

Wealth and Security

Bhisma stated that the duty of the citizens is to welcome a king. A kingless state is a weak state and bound to face the atrocities of the robbers. (Shantiparva, Ch. 67, Sloka 2).

It is, therefore, protection of material wealth for which people needs a powerful government.

Moreover, a state without an authoritative head is a disgrace. The people there do not care for protection of their dharma or righteous roles and duties and instead try to harm others. (Ch. 67, 3).

No one is safe in a ruler less state. In a state like this, even Agni, the Fire God does not carry the ritualistic sacrifice for the gods by the devotees. (Shantiparva, 67, 5).

Thus it signifies that people are not able to perform their spiritual duties properly in a kingless state. Any spiritual activities need a peaceful environment as well as economic stability. Economic stability cannot be achieved without proper administration.

And if any powerful king of another state invades, it is wise to welcome him properly and support him because it is nothing worse than a kingless state lost to anarchy. (Shantiparva, 67, 6-7)

In a state without any ruler, the wicked persons grab other people's wealth and enjoy. But when other people take away their possessions, they desire for a king. In a kingless state, two people conspire to grab another's wealth and many other people then take away this two person's wealth. The wicked people forcibly make some persons who are not to be made slave as slave. The wrongdoers also kidnap other people's wives. For all these reasons the gods created rules for a welfare seeking king who protects his subjects (Shantiparva, 67, 13-15)

The king is at the center of all righteousness performed by the subjects. Due to the fear of the king, they cannot become jealous of one another. (Shantiparva 68, 8). Without a king, the thieves could snatch valuables even from one's hand. (Shantiparva68, 28) When the head of a state is fully able to protect the state, women can go anywhere in the state wearing all their ornaments. (Shantiparva 68, 31-32)

Peace and Harmony

Bhisma stated that people live in harmony in a society when there is a king. He explained it with imageries. He said that in absence of the sun and the moon, people cannot see each other in the deep darkness. Without a big fish in a pond, the small fishes quarrel with each other which subsequently leads to their perish. Similarly without any fear from wild animals, the birds in a forest even cannot tolerate each other. They attack each other and die at last. And without a ruler, the citizens also suffer and perish (Shantiparva, 68, 14). Through the imageries, Bhisma has pointed out the exigency of a king.

Moreover, just like people can sleep peacefully with their main gates closed, people can move fearlessly everywhere with the protection of the king (Shantiparva, 68,30)

And people care for one another and do not become jealous of other when the state gives overall security (Shantiparva, 68, 33)

Property and Possession

The Law of property supplies the legal framework for allocating resources and distributing wealth. From a legal viewpoint, property is a bundle of rights. These rights describe what people may or may not do with the resources they own. These rights may change from one generation to another (Cooter and Ulen, 2004). However, people and societies disagree sharply about how to allocate resources and distribute wealth.

Right of property is a subject which never fails to strike the imagination of the intelligentsia. The philosophers generally perceive property to be an instrument for pursuing fundamental values. Bentham defines property as an expectation of utility. The Utilitarians measure the value of a good or an act by the net pleasure or satisfaction that it creates. For utilitarians, the purpose of the institution of property is to maximise the total pleasure or satisfaction obtained from material and other resources. Another philosophical approach to property law emphasises property law's ability to achieve distributive justice, rather than pleasure or satisfaction. For Aristotle, the principle of justice is different for different societies, but it is appropriate for each type of society to promote its own conception of distributive justice through its constitution and laws, including its notion of property rights. He argued that a democracy will favour an equal distribution of wealth, whereas an aristocracy, the form preferred by Aristotle will favour the distribution of wealth according to the virtues of the different classes. In Aristotle's conception, it is just that aristocrats receive an unequal share of wealth because they use it for more worthy ends than do others. Besides utility and distributive justice, another value that may underline property law is liberty. Hegel stressed the idea that people, through their works, transform nature into an expression of personality, and by doing so perfect the natural world. A painter takes materials in no particular order and rearrange them into a work of art. By investing personality in work, the artist transforms natural objects and makes them the artist's own. It is difficult to imagine a system of property law that did not recognise the fact. Thus to encourage self-expression, the state needs to recognise the creators' rights of ownership over their creation. Another philosophical tradition focuses not on the purposes of property but on its origins. To illustrate, in medieval times there were many encumbrances and restrictions on the use and sale of real estate. The common law of private property emerged from feudalism and acquired its modern character by chipping away of these encumbrances on the marketability of the real property. Political conservatives like Burke and Hayek idealise forms of social order that, like the common law of property, evolve over time in much the same manner as the myriad species of life.

Bhisma thus in the Shantiparva has highlighted the need for government for protection of private property. Without protection from the king, the head of the state in the Mahabharata society, no one can have any possession over anything on earth, be it over his wife, children, foods and other consumables or over any other materials. Without security from a king, all wealth ultimately perish (68,15). It is claimed in the Shantiparva that without security from the king, the thieves and robbers would have forcibly taken all the material wealth, be it jewellery, precious stones, cars and clothes from everyone (68, 16).

Without a king, the wrongdoers overpower the right doers and everyone ultimately accept the immoral actions. (Shantiparva 68, 17) Without a king the wealthy citizens always face the threat of life and property for being wealthy. Nobody can claim any material as their own (Shantiparva 68, 19).

Thus according to the Mahabharata a stateless society existed where love was universal and life was happy. This reminds us of the state of nature as delineated by Rousseau. According to Rousseau, the trouble begins when the notion of private property cropped up. And it seems that the Mahabharata agrees with Rousseau. The Mahabharata posits that with the advent of private property there was the necessity of the ruler. All this happened with the decline of the Satyayuga. Since the ruler protects the private property of the individuals, he or she is capable of imposing unequal distribution among the masses where there is a big chasm between the rich and the poor. At the same time the ruler can do away with the gap between the haves and the have nots. And property rights are efficient when they create incentives to maximise a nation' resource. Property rights also maximise wealth by making the owner internalise the benefits and costs of using a resource. The role of an able ruler should be guided by these factors.

Protection of Respected and Dependent People

Everyone could torture their old parents, teachers and guests. They could even kill the weak if there were no king (Shantiparva 68, 18). In the Mahabharata society, the Brahmins were highly respected for their nobility of character. So to kill a Brahmin was a sacrilege. And may be a good person being scandalised by the event of a Brahmin being killed might kill one who had killed the Brahmin. But that would be taking the law in one's own hand. Hence the necessity of a government that might adjudicate on such issues (Shantiparva 68, 27).

Longevity of the Citizens

A king protects his subjects. Unless they are secure under the protecting umbrella of the king, the citizens are bound to suffer untimely death. This was not true only in the days of the Mahabharata but very much relevant in the world today. Kerala for example, in India today, provided fairly reliable basic health care decades earlier. Consequently life expectation in Kerala shot up and Kerala became relatively prosperous than other states in India (Sen, pg xlvii). If there were no good administration, the whole state would go under the clutch of the dacoits and everyone would suffer untold misery (68, 20).

This reminds us of the state of Nature as delineated by Hobbes where life was nasty and brutish and dull.

Protection of Livelihood of the Citizens

Agriculture or trade cannot survive without a state head. The Vedas which are the storehouse of thoughts of greatest intellectuals could perish. Dharma would not prevail (Shantiparva 68, 22). History has been witness to the destruction of libraries at Taxila, Nalanda, Alexdandria and so on. This testifies the truth of Shantiparva. The ultimate objective in ancient Indian philosophy is to achieve the freedom from material bondage. But this cannot be achieved bypassing material needs. Man must live two hundred percent, hundred percent physically and hundred percent spiritually. Hence one must attend to worldly duties and chores. According to Varna system of ancient Indian society, the economy sustains when one diligently performs the assigned functions according to the social norms. However without the careful supervision of the king, it could not be possible. The students, the disciples, the ascetics and the Brahmins no one could study seriously the four Vedas without a strong state head (Shantiparva 68, 26)

When a king protects his citizens, the citizens of all Varnas, engage in different economic activities perform Yajnas and rituals for gods and concentrate on their studies. (Shantiparva 68, 34)

Yajna

The ritual of Yajna is designed to establish man's connection with the cosmic properies abounding in the universe.

In the Bhagavad Gita Lord Krishna says to Arjuna:

Annādbhavantibhūtāni
Parjanyādanna-sambhavaḥ
Yajñādbhavatiparjanyo
Yajñaḥ karma-samudbhavaḥ
Bhagavad Gita (3.14)

All living beings spring forth from Anna or food which is a product of rain. Rain is caused by yajna, the sacrificial fire ceremony which in turn takes place due to karma or action.

Yajna thus does not just mean a ritual where pooja items are consigned to the flames and dedicated to the gods. The word yajna consists of three syllables – ya, ja and na, which refer to the three processes involved in every act we perform – production (ya), distribution (ja) and assimilation (na). There has to be a balance between these three components. Sharing one's wealth with other members of society is of topmost value (Gyanshruti, 2006). In Sanskrit dravya means wealth. Wealth has an associated power. Money as wealth has purchasing power. Health as wealth is physical power. Knowledge as wealth is the power of comprehension. The desire to donate all that one possesses for the benefit of others is performing Yajna at every moment.

Yajna therefore induces self-development. Righteous behaviour and sacrificial principles are the most needed attributes for creating a harmonious and benevolent society.

Thus Yajna is a means of remaining on the righteous path in order to lead a purposeful life.

The ritualistic sacrifice ceremonies the Yajna, marriage or any social duty could not be done without a king. (Shantiparva 68, 22, 68, 25). Yajna is very significant from different perspectives, be it the distribution of wealth, be it exchange of thought among the enlightened ones and be it the occasion of a show of strength of the organiser of the ceremony. So there should not be any obstruction in the smooth functioning of the ceremony. And it needs huge money power, man power as well as reputation to organise a big Yajna ceremony.

Cow Rearing and Protection

The bulls and cows cannot do their normal procreation functions without the able supervision of a ruler. And thus the Cowherds would not survive for long without their wealth – the cow (Shantiparva 68, 23). Cow was treated as a wealth in the Mahabharata society and therefore cow rearing was considered to be an important activity in the economy of the Mahabharata society.

Good Governance

Lawlessness could be everywhere without an administrator. Famine would have been a regular occurrence (Shantiparva 68, 29). It is claimed that the three Vedas protect the universe. And it is the good governance which protects all the Vedas (Shantiparva 68, 35)

Imagery Used for Good Governance

If the king with his sceptre is not able to protect the state and its people, then the powerful inhabitants would kill all the poor ones just like a big fish that lives in water and eats all the small fishes. (Shantiparva 67, 16)

Good Governance – The Views in the Adiparva of the Mahabharata

Not only in the Shantiparva, the necessity of an efficient ruler and good governance is a recurrent topic, for discussion, in different chapters of the Mahabharata. For instance, in the Adiparva the first chapter, King Parikshit, the grandson of the Pandavas did a great wrong. He put a dead snake on the meditating sage Shamik as he thought that the sage ignored him. The son of the sage became angry. He cursed the king that on the seventh day, the famous snake Takshak would bite him. The sage Shamik however scolded his son. He explained that a king even if he did some wrong should be pardoned. It is the king who protects the sages. Without a king, the sages could not perform their functions to protect the dharma. With protection from a righteous minded king, the sages earn their virtues. Therefore the king is a part of their virtue and a king should be forgiven even if he does a wrongful act. (Mahabharata Adiparva, 41, 22-24)

It is claimed in the Shantiparva that a state without a ruler suffers from many problems like danger from robbers. When the citizens become undisciplined, the king enforces law to discipline them. When people get scared of the sceptre, peace prevails everywhere. This shows the efficacy of showing fear and threats of punishment. If people always remain angry, they cannot perform their roles. Thus the king is the centre of the dharma and dharma brings eternal happiness. So when the king performs his righteous duties, the happy gods give rains. The rain creates crops and people are sustained (Adiparva, 41, 27-30)

The king protects the state and so the king is the father of the citizen or pater familias. And the great sage Manu stated that a king is equivalent to ten of the highest respected Brahmins (Mahabharata, 41, 31).

Thus, Bhisma's discourse on the necessity of a king is based widely on the economic grounds. Without an effective government, the creation, preservation and proper distribution of wealth cannot take place. The lust for wealth brings the consequences like lawlessness, war, hamper of economic activities like trade, agriculture and cow rearing. And the most important of all is that the Yajna or the ritualistic sacrifice, the foundation of the Mahabharata society could not be possible without the supervision of the king.

5

Shantiparva – Some Notes

The canvas of the book Shantiparva is vast. Through discourses, questions and answers, case studies of good and bad kings in the form of narratives, the propositions in the forms of wisdom are explicated. The economic thoughts of the Mahabharata as explicated in the Shantiparva needs to be identified as a distinct identity. It has its own paradigm. Its unique lessons are useful to look at many problems in an alternative way. The concluding chapter summarises some lessons significant from the standpoint of study of the 'whole'. For instance, the modern economics has its limitedness in differentiating between economic and non-economic activities, between work time and leisure. However the ancient Indian political philosophical thoughts consider the society as a whole. There is organic relation between the so called productive and unproductive people in the present market based economic system. The unproductive section, many a times, emanates from the forces of competition in the market. In this context, the present study touches upon a so called unproductive people – the beggars. The topic of begging is a frequent one in the Shantiparva. A beggar in Oxford dictionary means a person, typically a homeless one, who lives by asking for money or food.

A common proverb is that beggars cannot be choosers. In other words people with no other options must be content with what is offered. A beggar is not considered as an economic man in the mainstream economics. A beggar is an outlier. The person is not a part of production system and does not add any value in production. The person is only a consumer who has no option of choice. And many of them even are homeless. Since the market based economic system fails to bring them under its chain, the so called developed western civilisation termed these beggars as an unproductive one. They are treated as parasites.

And indeed begging opens the raw fact of unequal distribution of wealth in a society. It is poverty which is considered the main reason for helpless people to beg. The Times of India reported that "India has 3.72 lakh beggars of whom 21% are literate, having passed senior secondary certificate exams and above. In fact, more than 3,000 of them have professional diplomas, or are graduates and even post-graduates, according to the Census 2011 data on 'Non-workers by main activity and education level'. Many of them have turned the adage 'Beggars cannot be choosers' on its head – especially considering they are literate but chose beggary after their degrees failed to land them satisfactory jobs (*The Times of India*, Dec 31, 2015).

However begging has a wider interpretation in India, apart from its worldly meaning, begging has a spiritual interpretation. In India's spiritual tradition, begging or *Bhiksha* was a way of seeking spiritual wealth. And spiritual wealth which is search for liberation or moksha is the ultimate freedom from worldly bondages. The ancient Indian literatures especially Ramayana and the Mahabharata do not consider begging as a hateful activity. And in Buddhist philosophy, Lord Buddha referred to his monks as Bhikkhu.

In the Shantiparva of the Mahabharata, The grief stricken Yudhisthira, after the Great War, told Arjuna that if they had to choose to beg at the cities ruled by other Kshyatriya clans, the Pandavas would have been spared from the killing of their own relatives. Yudhisthira lamented that for greed of wealth and power, they killed their own friends. So he wanted to dispose of all his property, kingdom and to survive on begging. He resolved not to judge the quality of the food received as alms. He made up his mind to beg his food from the head of the first house and if he is refused there, he would go to the second one and in case of further refusal, he decided to seek his alms from the third one and in this way he would try up to the seventh one. After cooking the food and distributing among the beggars, he would take the residue only once in the day. However, wife Draupadi and his brothers countered his argument. They reminded him that a king could not abandon his role to be a beggar. And moreover, a householder also cannot abandon his duties for his family and the larger society to become a beggar. A householder and a king are considered to be the provider of sustenance to the beggars.

Begging indicates the importance of charity in India's sociology and economic system. A human being is not always a selfish rational person with its own bundle of worldly demands. He has some altruistic desires. Giving alms is a way of fulfilling that desire.

Again begging also teaches an alternative way of living. It is how to live without any option of worldly choice of what to eat or drink. One is not constrained by the pressure of nonsense abundance of choices. More choices sometimes create more confusion among the prospective buyers of a good or service. And one can have a second thought about begging which in other words is to be satisfied with minimum.

Thus beggars seem to be choosers of an alternative way of living based on welfare, charity and the minimum needs criteria.

The issue which deserves special mention is how the notion of time is explored in the Shantiparva. Yudhisthira speaks his heart to Sage Vyasdeva. He is feeling guilty and is in deep repentance. He feels responsible for the wailing of all the bereaved women who lost their husbands and sons in the Kurukshetra war. Vyasdeva consoles him and advises him to accept that nothing can bring back the fleeting breath because that is the law of Nature. Vyasdeva through the tale of Senjit explains the significance of right time. Without right time, no endeavour can succeed. This advice is very significant for any economic pursuit. Senjit once told that a difficult time cycle affects every people, and everything is perishable. When the wife or a son or the parents die, wealth erodes, everyone plunges into sorrow. But one's body is not his or her own and the world is also not one's private property. Again, from another perspective the body and the world belong to one and everyone. Sorrow is never ending and joy sustains a very short life. Joy and woe follow each other. So, one who is in search of permanent peace should be free from both the feeling of joy and woe. Senjit said that if one behaves with his wife and son with less composure, one could know the actual relationship between them. Nobody could be happy or unhappy for any event.

Time management tends to become a discipline thanks to the evolution of a new digital socio economic world. The right time concept of the natural world as discussed in the Mahabharata is based around agricultural activities that involve human interaction with Nature. Time in natural world is related to astronomical and biological factors. But the so-called new industrial revolution or the internet revolution has changed the natural work – leisure pattern of life (vide Dr. Chandana Mitra in her article "Cultural lag in respect of youth and digital world" (*Platform*, December 2018).

The duty of a king is to take initiative for war, to fight, to use his policy of punishment with justice, to give donations and remunerations to the deserving ones in Yajna. And a king who obeys these duties is a pure one. The king who is just and competent to rule his state, performs Yajna, egoless, looks after his subjects according to dharma, protects his state by winning in war, looks after his subjects by performing Somayajna, justly punish, learns Vedas properly, care for people of all the four classes in their own dharmas, such a king enjoys eternal respect and peace. And in the context of Vyasdeva's teachings we might posit that wealth is not retrieved unless the right time is there.

Shantiparva focuses on the Vedic philosophy of distribution of wealth. Arjuna said to Yudhisthirathat there is nothing greater than money (artha) and a penniless one does not get heavenly peace or wealth. Yudhisthira cites the famous discourse of king Yayati in this context. Yayati once said that one who does not scare anybody and one who is not afraid of anyone else, one who is neither interested nor disinterested in any worldly comfort achieves Brahman – the infinite. When one abandons all attachment to any living creature one achieves Brahman. The self-aware individual who controls his mind and desires, and the self-contented one who discards any association with sense objects can achieve liberation – moksha easily.

Yudhisthira reminds Arjuna that for a person who works for the sake of money, it is very difficult for him to forsake his work. A person, who is devoid of good conduct, controlled by woe and fear, carried off by a little desire for wealth and not worried about the sin he commits can do awful harm to others.

Lord Brahmaa, the Creator, created wealth for Yajna and created people for protection of Yajna. Yajna in Indian culture is considered a noble activity for the benefit of the whole existence. Wealth should be used only for Yajna – the sacrificial worship. It should not be used for fulfilling lust. The people who are respected should use their wealth for donation and Yajna. Surplus wealth should be donated. And Bhisma prescribes the norms of donation. Wealth should not be given to any unworthy ones and the worthy ones should get it properly.

As things stand today in order to achieve sustainable peace the role and function of the government is very significant. Economic policies are largely depended on the politics pursued by different states. So a word or two as to the role of the government will not be out of place where economics is largely looked upon as political economy.

In the ancient Indian political economic thoughts, king is synonymous with the state and the government. Kautilya, the pioneer of the field of political science and economics in India says in the Arthashastra the ancient Indian political treatise that "the people of a society, whatever their *varna* or stage of life, will follow their own *dharma* and pursue with devotion their occupations, if they are protected by the king and if there is the just use of *danda*" (*Coercion and Punishment* 1.4.16)

Dandaniti or the science of law enforcement is dwelled on in the Shantiparva of the Mahabharata. Bhisma, the protagonist in the Shantiparva stated that in the state of Nature, the institutions of state did not exist. This implies that the absence of the King coincided with the absence of private property. When the individual was living in that utopian stage, he was dictated by the dictates of law of nature and everyone was living a very blissful life. The problem emerged with the advent of private property. Later on because of the demand of peace and security, the need for an authority figure has been felt. The theory of punishment (Danda) is advanced as a political theory implying the science of Government.

In the Shantiparva, the chapter on peace of the Mahabharata, the greatest importance has been given everywhere to the State and its constituents. The king's duty is assumed to be the establishment of social harmony, without which he cannot administer the State. The State must create conditions which are conducive to the achievement of peace and harmony.

The study ends with some notes. It is not possible in a single study for a close reading of all of them. However, they remind us the present inhabitants of the world, how to live a worthy life with the judicious use of wealth.

Some of the Observations are summarised below

War has many consequences. And nothing is more devastating than the plight of the close ones and the dependents of the war martyrs. War is masculine. The killed ones are termed as martyrs and the winners are war heroes. But, the war widows remain only a theme for the poets and compassionate people in the society. Even today, we shed our tears when we see the grieving picture of the bereaved wife whose soldier husband has been killed in any border conflict in his duty to save the motherland or fatherland. But their plight never ever helped to end the violence in any part of the world, be it in the Mahabharata times and be it in the present century.

Vyasdeva reminds Yudhisthira that those who are killed in the war cannot be alive again. It shows that one should be responsible for the consequence of one's act beforehand. There is no meaning to lament when all is said and done. Wealth can be gained and lost. But life is more precious than wealth, because a dead person cannot be alive again. However without our focus on this value judgement, we continue to remain engaged in activities for fulfilling the contingent desires and demands. And economics, the study of household thus turned to a study of money only. Money becomes greater than life itself.

Each and every sub chapters of the Shantiparva has something to note. The conversations of the four Pandava brothers along with Yudhisthira regarding the utility of money and power can be called the first debate in any literature on economics.

The following notes are some instances:

- Arjuna's speech reveals the significance of money in the society.
- Arjuna stated that the wealth of a wealthy person multiplies. And in today's economy, there are ample evidences that money attracts money.
- Arjuna clearly explains what the word 'weak' means in a society. Lack of physical strength is not the only example of weakness. A penniless person is also considered a weak one in the society he belongs to.
- Arjuna is also very clear about the takeoff situation. It is the distribution of the wealth for the welfare of the mass which results in the takeoff. So take off – Abhyudaya is not the maximisation of wealth collection, rather it the distribution of the wealth of the king for the welfare of the mass which should be the foremost duty of a king. Arjuna's counselling to Yudhisthira citing a past event signifies Foucalt's 'polyhedron of intelligibilty'. By this

Focault meant that we can only really understand something-it only became intelligible by looking at it from different directions and using different methods.

- The chapter on peace stresses the importance of sacrifice. And sacrifice means detachment from the wealth one possesses. It does not mean that one who should not engage in his activities to acquire wealth or one should not use them for survival. But it means one should look after his family as well as should distribute his wealth to the persons whom the society thinks fit for distribution.
- The discourse of Nakula, Sahadeva and Draupadi state what a king's ideal role should be. Draupadi's preaching reveals her in depth knowledge about the administrative duties of a king. She has idea about the role of an ideal king as well as the territorial jurisdiction of Yudhisthira. She knows about the revenue sources of king Yudhisthira. She also thinks that a king should not be an ascetic, but to act wisely according to the situations and donate wealth through Yajna. Food is vital for sustenance. One who provides food is one who gives life. This is a priceless statement of queen Draupadi, the strong character of the Mahabharata.
- The advices given toYudhisthiraregarding the importance of Yajnas and especially Ashwamedha Yajnas to getrid of his mental agony. The Shatpath Brahmana (13.1.6) defines AshwamedhaYajna as 'Rashtramva Ashwamedha'. It implies that the true meaning of the term Ashwamedha is to administer and manage the state in an efficient manner. Thus it was performed as a symbol of good governance where the

needs of the subjects were considered and addressed with due care and responsibility. The predominant form of Ashwamedha sacrifice is followed by the free release of the horse that was worshipped and honoured during the sacrifice. Carrying the royal insignia of the king who performed the sacrifice, the horse shall move forth unhindered. It is assumed that the regions where the horse set its foot accepted the supremacy of the king who sent it. In case someone wanted to challenge his supremacy, they might capture the horse and tie. It means they are ready for a war with the king who sent the horse (Sathya Narayanan "Ashwamedh Yajna", speakingtree.in, December 24, 2015). The sacrificial ceremonies are also of many types. The Rajasuya Yajna is a yajna which means sacrifices worth for a king or it is of such a huge scale which only a king is able to perform. In the Aswamedha Yajna sacrifice of a horse is a ritual. In sacrificial distribution ceremonies, the recipients were mainly Brahmins though it was mentioned in some stories that nobody was barred from entry there. Aswamedha Yajna: Vyasdeva asserts that performance of this Yajna gives peace of mind. And a unique feature of this Yajna is that a king who organises this ceremony goes to different states, the kings of those states can either obey him as the one who conquers their kingdom or can refuse to let off the organiser's horse and declare a war. However, the winner king ultimately appoints the deceased or defeated king's relatives as his representative. In Mahabharata there is thus no description of any post war torture or violence in the states defeated by war.

- The role of punishment is considered to be a significant one for public administration in the Shantiparva. With vivid examples of different activities Arjuna states that how punishment is sine qua non for a smooth society. He also agrees that violence is embedded in each and every action. The nature of punishment is related to the Varnas i.e. with the socio economic structure. A punishment given to the Brahmins differ from that to the Kayastha and so on. Arjuna's explanation in support of punishment and violence reinstate the famous statement "Fair is foul and foul is fair". The word Punishment on the surface seems foul but it is sine qua non for smooth functioning of the world. Vyasa tells a story of two brothers. From that story one can learn many lessons. The significant duty of a king is the wise use of his right to punish. And it seems that if a kingor any administrator performs this duty efficiently, the common people should have faith in him. The commoners then shun their own violent methods to take law in their own hands and respect the verdict of their authority. And the offenders would be afraid to do any wrong due to fear of stringent punishment. The effect would be a bountiful economy with close bonding among the members of the society shunning any violence.

- According to Yudhisthira, a happy person is one who is free from any material desire. An index of happiness can be constructed from his view where happiness can be placed with as an inverse relationship with the variables like anger, anxiety, discontent, stupidity, emotions and yearning for material possessions. Economics of happiness is a much discussed topic now a day. One can get an idea of what is meant by happiness in the Mahabharata text.

- Yudhisthira's quote of saint king Janaka is a significant one. First of all, it was the opinions of the common men of Yudhisthira's about Janaka, who reigned at an earlier time period. So the quote establishes the fact how common men of that time values the perception about a king's wealth and how they valued the opinion of a king in this context. The king's wealth is not one's private property. So one should not have any personal attachment or possessiveness to it. Arjuna's narration of another story about Janaka is also the tale of common men about Janaka. And it is a conversation between the king and the queen. It is interesting that the conversation between a king and a queen regarding the duties of a king and what it actually means to be a sage becomes a historical tale.
- From the Shantiparva, we are getting the perception about one's wealth not only during the Mahabharata time but also of the pre Mahabharata time period through different tales. And these tales which here is narrated are transmitted from one time era to another era through oral histories. And the historians are the common people. And so the stories are in a nutshell granaries of economic and ethical thoughts of the ruler as well as the ruled, the emperor and the common men. There are prescribed norms of how one should donate the surplus wealth. There is also the question of the right person who needs it, the right attitude of the donor and so on. Arjuna once states that one who is a pauper cannot be able to arrange sacrificial ceremonies to please the gods. And thus he cannot attain infinite peace or

material wealth. However, Yudhisthira opposes this view. According to Yudhisthira, what matters most is the right attitude to life. One should not seek wealth for the sake of wealth. Wealth should be earned only for proper distribution. One should not hoard it and use it for satisfying lust. Shantiparva describes in details the right attitude to wealth, how to produce, distribute and consume it for one's own satisfaction and for which is beneficial to the society as a whole.

- The focus is on peace. And here it is explained clearly by Vyasdeva that doing one's duty lawfully is the only way to achieve eternal peace.
- The philosopher sages of the Mahabharata society were no less aware of the material world. The advices some in form of stories gives some best lessons about an ideal economic system and the desirable leadership. The advanced capitalist system is concerned about the surplus production. To distribute the surplus, they are finding new ways to colonise countries. And in this plethora of newer and newer goods day by day, people are getting confused, more lustful and increasingly dissatisfied of what they already have. Is there any alternative form of surplus distribution? The sages of Mahabharata guide us. They did not advise to abandon all the designated duties and to go to forest. They say one should do their duties as expected from them, stay in their families but should distribute their surplus i.e. their savings earned by honest activities for the society through Yajna. A king was expected to observe the four stages of life as mentioned in the Vedic stage. The four stages of life of a person were connected with the

production, distribution, consumption and welfare of the society.

- There were specific ways of life for different castes based on what they do in the society. A Kshatriya, the warrior class should not live on other's earning. One's caste was not judged primarily for his worthiness. It was mainly his nature of activities, the main determinant of his/her worthiness. Arjuna cited the story of Lord Indra here to establish that fact. And above all activities, the most important one was sacrifices. So at the root of all actions, thoughts of welfare economics seem to be the inherent one. One cannot be oblivious of the others. People were free to choose whether they would work or not. Thus it was a truly free economic system under the able administration of a monarch.
- One can be aware that how knowledgeable and compassionate the intellectual teachers were of the Mahabharata society. Vyasa did not forget to mention the role of a head of the family in providing sustenance even to the other inhabitants of the nature. Today we suddenly become environment conscious after all is said and done. Vyasa states that a king should be blamed for a drought if he remains inactive to prevent it. Moreover he also mentions how an insensitive government is responsible for stealing and robbery.
- The stalwarts who were counselling Yudhisthira did not claim that they were themselves authority on any subject. They advised with the instance of similar subjects of earlier histories. It is like the secondary data we use in our research studies. Vyasdeva the all knower also recounts the Manu's philosophy to explain

Yudhisthira the ideal way of life. Thus it is inherent in Hindu philosophy from the prehistorical past.

- The Mahabharata is history of histories of different ages. And these histories focus not only on victories but also how a king should be a name not only during his lifetime but also long after his death. The focus is more on how a monarch with immense material wealth distributes it through sacrificial ceremonies. The more able an administrator, the more bountiful is the Nature. The ancient histories depicted in Mahabharata tell us that in a reign of a good monarch, people also are free from any danger, untimely death and accidents. All the economic activities of that time, be it agriculture, animal husbandry or trade everything runs on smoothly. Every monarch ruled for a long time. Thus people it seems had higher life expectancies.
- The girls were treated as wealth. And thus they could be donated as wealth. Dowry was prevalent among the kings. But a king who was a benevolent one donates them through sacrificial distribution ceremonies. Besides gold, the animals like elephants, horses and cows were also treated as wealth. One can violate the rules of the dharma in greed of wealth. And it is the dharma of the Kshatyias, the warriors to punish them. Thus, the dharma of the warrior class is to protect other's dharma. Wealth is not only jewels. What is a wealth or not depends on the time concerned. Six types of wealth are mentioned in this discourse which were mainly wealth during war times in the ancient scriptures
- A king's dharma – moral responsibilities imply to destroy the wicked ones, to donate to the worthies and

to protect his subjects. Who is a wicked one and who is a worthy one is also determined by dharma.

- Warfare is generally associated with violence and destruction of life. However, the necessity of war is interpreted in a unique way in Mahabharata. The creator of Mahabharata, on the surface, is not a preacher of anti-war or nonviolence. But, the necessity of killing is interpreted in a deeper way. One suffers no sin if he kills one for the peace and happiness of the masses. Thus it is assumed that other people will never engage in misdeeds. Because if any other further do any wicked ones, he will face the same fate and so on. Thus killing, a brutal act is used as an administrative policy to combat more violence or to bring peace. So peace seems to be a fruit of violence.
- There is a deeper interpretation of any action. An action can be on the surface an immoral one, but actually a moral one and vice versa. However, it seems that morality or immorality is considered from the viewpoint of the powerful ones – the kings or the gods. There is no subaltern interpretation of what good activity is and what a malicious activity is. And a king's dharma is to protect his state. The classifications of moral and immoral activities are context based. No activity seems to be unpardonable. Everyone can be free of sins with suitable remedial measures. Among the remedial measures, donation takes a high place. So, one with abundant money wealth seems to be more powerful in the society. They can incur in more sins.
- However, the philosopher teachers assured that one can be free of his/her evil deeds with his own efforts and

penance. Even if there are no remedial measures in the shastras, one could still follow the methods of self-refinement through control of his senses and achieving self-knowledge consequently.

- The Mahabharata looks upon life as a continuous one with link to its past, present and future after death. Thus how a man should behave is also mentioned. One should be humble. And longevity, a necessary one to perform all the good activities in a life span is essential. Dharma and adharma – good and evil are context based. Their interpretations are different for different time periods and in different counties. A good deed can be an evil one in some circumstances and vice versa. A good deed is one whose ultimate result is good and vice versa – the cause and effect relation – a deed is good when a good cause leads to a good effect. Again when we see the ultimate effect is good, we can justify it as a good effort. There are even remedial measures for immoral activities one performs knowingly. And interestingly though the king is all powerful to give punishment, even if king pardons a person but the person knows he is guilty he could be free from his sins through remedial penance. And this rule is also applicable to the king himself. A king is advised by a priest when required. And in the absence of a priest, he can purify himself by fasting.

- Food is a basic requirement for sustenance. And the stress is given on the person whose food is not to be taken, who offers it and the quality of the food, the preparation method, and the economic activities of the server. It is rather a food guide. When it is mentioned that one should not eat a food prepared by a new mother with a new born child of ten days, it seems that it is a way of protecting both mother and child. The mother thus gets some time to recuperate and nurse her baby. This is same for the cow also. Similarly a food prepared for dead one is prepared with a different frame of mind and should be taken.. Some professions are mentioned from whom food should not be taken. It seems they are not considered a respectable one by Manu. Though to the present reader, it seems that they are very necessary to the society. It is said that one should eat from a person who gives loan. Then what will happen to people who need money during emergency as well as for a business purpose? In present market economy, there is no concept of free lunch. A person who gives loan should deserve an interest for the money he gives as loan. It is mentioned not to take food from a characterless woman. This is also a debatable one as what does one means by a character of a woman. Moreover it is said that one should not eat from a gambler. But Yudhisthira himself was a gambler who has staked even his wife in gambling. Thus what Manu stated and what Vyasdeva says to the king Yudhisthira seems contradictory even during Yudhisthira's time.

- Yudhisthira regained the mental peace he lost after the devastation of Kurukshetra war. It was due to wise advice of the saints and Lord Krishna. It is a lesson for the war-ravaged world even today to get rid of the depression, evil thoughts and to the penance for the welfare of the masses.

- A king should be a level headed one. And he should be an example to everybody. Revenge does not mean only bloodshed. Revenge is sweeter and worthier when one gives service to the person who is the cause of suffering at some point of time. Dharma, artha and kama are assumed to be inseparable parts of the state administration. An administrator cannot afford to be emotional and nonviolent. He must do his duty. The qualities of a king are the guidelines for the top managers of any organisation or those who are in leadership position. A leader is one who motivates his or her followers. He should inculcate some praiseworthy characteristics. Shantiparva discusses some behavioural norms required to be successful in any endeavour.

- Peace prevails when the citizens are aware of their duties. A successful governance is best judged from the attitudes of the citizens being governed.
- There are advices for how to deal with adverse time. There is no concept of nationality here. One can leave his native place if the situation permits that. The story of a hunter and a pigeon couple is a moral teaching of how one should treat a helpless refugee who begs for shelter. The pigeon couple sacrificed their own lives for feeding a cruel hunter. And that changed the outlook of the hunter who then had sacrificed his own life. And all of them went to heaven after death. Bhisma explains that protecting a helpless refugee is a very pious act. One can compare the outlook with the attitude of most of the countries where influx of refugees is now a major concern

At the end of the chapter on peace, Yudhisthira is eager to learn that what should be the right behaviour of a person so that he achieves freedom from sorrow and move happily in this world? Bhisma narrates an old history – the conversation between Prahlada and Ajagar Saint. Ajagarbrata is to follow the life of a python. A python does not move hard to get its food.

For me a researcher whose objective of studying Shantiparva from the viewpoint of economic thoughts and principles of management finds the chapter an immensely significant one in the present context. A Brahmin who wanted to do greatest dharma ritual on advice of his guest went to the king of the snakes, listened from him the merits of leading a frugal life Yudhisthira wants to know what is the greatest dharma for people who observe the ashramadharma. One earns the highest merit when one survives by eating seeds and roots from the soil, eat frugal and observes Yama-niyama

Note

It is the end of the Shantiparva. Does it mean that peace lies in sustaining only with what nature gives us willingly?

Bibliography

Primary Sources

Bhattacharya, Madhusudan. (Banggabda1316, year 1909AD). *Ratnamala* (First Volume in Bengali). (n.d.)

Goenka, J. (ed). Bandyopadhyaya, Gayatri (translated in Bengali). (n.d.) *Samkhipta Mahabharata (1st and 2nd Vol) (Concise Mahabharata)*. Gorakhpur: Gita Press.

Mullick, Pramatha Nath. (n.d.). *The Mahabharata As It Was, Is And Shall Be.* Kolkata: Pioneer Press.

Omkarnath, Shri Shri Sitaramadas. (Banggabda 1380, Year 1973 AD). *Aryashastra, Mahabharata, Shantiparva*. Kolkata: Shri Sitaram Vedic Mahavidyalaya.

Subramaniam, Kamala. (1997). *Mahabharata*, Mumbai: Bharatiya Vidya Bhaban.

Secondary Sources

Ahuja, Ram. (2009). *Indian social system*. Jaipur: Rawat Publications.

Bokare, M. G. (1993). *Hindu Economics*. Pune: M. G. Bokare Memorial Foundation.

Cooter. R. and Ulen, Thomas. (2004). *Law and Economics*, Fourth Edition, Pearson Education.

Das, S. K. (1937). *The Economic History of Ancient India.* Published by S. K. Das.

Dasgupta, Ajit Kumar. (1993). *A History of Indian Economic Thought.* London: Routledge.

Dhand, Arti. (2002). "The dharma of ethics, the ethics of dharma." *Journal of Religious Ethics,* 347-372.

Dominic, K. V. (2011). *Write Son, Write-A Collection of Poems.* New Delhi: GNOSIS.

Ghosh, Mousumi. (2018, June). "Treasury and Wealth in Management – The Economic Thoughts in the Shantiparva of the Mahabharata." *Platform – A bilingual Journal Based on Literature and Culture.*

.... (2018, December). "Chaturashrama and the Quality of Life." *Platform, A bilingual Journal Based on Literature and Culture.*

.... (2018). "Economic Thoughts and Principles of Management in the Shantiparva of the Mahabharata." *Proceedings of the 7th International Seminar on South Asian Literature in English, 14th and 15th December, 2018, Tamilnadu, Thiuvalluvar Government Arts College,* Chennai: Sri Krishna Publications.

.... (2019, January). "Cow A Wealth in the Ancient Indian Literature and Archetypal in Present Indian Literature." *International Journal on Multicultural Literature,* 9(1), 70-75.

.... (2019, January). "Economics of Peace and Harmony – Lessons from the Bhagavad Gita and the Shantiparva of the Mahabharata." *Culture and Quest.* ISISAR (International Society for Intercultural Studies and Research) Peace Research Publication.

.... (2019, January). "The Ideal State of Governance." *IJELLH (International Journal of English Language, Literature in Humanities) A UGC Approved Journal.* Sl. No: 43979, pages-58-62. [Full Paper presented in the UGC Sponsored National Seminar (13th and 14th August 2018, The Madura College)]

Hazari, Umakanta. (n.d.). *Vaidic Gavesana* (Vedic Research in Bengali), Kolkata.

http://literature.awgp.org/akhandjyoti/2005/May_Jun/v1.VedicCosmology_3 Searched on 10.12.18

https://en.wikipedia.org/wiki/Vyasa_searched on 9.12.18

Jary, David and Jary, Julia. (1991). *Collins Dictionary of Sociology.* Glasgow: Harper Collins.

Kautilya's *The Arthashastra*, Edited, Rearranged, Translated by L. N. Rangarajan. (1992). Penguin Books, India.

Kautilya's *The Arthashastra.* Edited by N C Bandyopadhyaya. (1927). Chakrabarty, Chatterjee and Co. Ltd., Calcutta.

Kautilya's *The Arthashastra*: Edited by R. P. Kangle. (1963). University of Bombay Press.

Kautilya's *The Arthashastra.* Edited by R. Shyamashastri. (1960). Mysore Printing and Publishing House, Mysore, 6th Edition.

Kosambi, Damodar Dharmananda. (1981). *The Culture and Civilisation of Ancient India*, New Delhi: Vikas Publishing House.

Levi-Strauss, C. (1979). *Myth and Meaning*, New York: Schocken Books.

"Mahabharata: Its status and retellings Chapter-II". Retrieved from shodhganga.inflibnet.ac.in

Matilal, Bimal Krishna. (Ed). (1989). *Moral Dilemmas in the Mahabharata.* Shimla: Indian Institute of Advanced Studies.

Mitra, Chandana. (2018, December). "Cultural lag in respect of youth and digital world." *Platformm – A bilingual Journal Based on Literature and Culture.*

Mukhopadhyaya, Ramesh Chandra. (2009). *Messages of God Men A Study of the Gitas in the Mahabharata*. Kolkata: Anjali Publishers.

.... (2008). *Rig Veda Samhita*, Kolkata: Underground Literature.

.... (2017). *K. V. Dominic Criticism and Commentary: Essential Readings Companion.* Ann Arbor: Modern History Press.

Polanyi, Karl. (2001). *The Great Transformation.* Boston: Beacon Press.

Radhakrishnan, S. (1948). *Religion and Society*. London: George. Allen and Unwin Ltd.

Renou, Louis. (1997). *The Civilisation in Ancient India.* New Delhi: Munshiram Manoharlal Publishers Pvt. Ltd.

Russel, B. (1960). *Principles of Social Reconstruction.* (1960). London: George Allen and Unwin Ltd, Fourteenth Impression.

Saha, Arunoday. (1993). "The caste system in India and its consequences." *International Journal of Sociology and Social Policy*, 1-76.

Sannyasi Gyanshruti and Sannyasi Srividyananda. (2006). *Yajna A Comprehensive Survey.* Munger Bihar: Yoga Publications Trust.

Sanyal, Sanjeev. (2012). *Land of The Seven Rivers*. Penguin Books, Page 51.

Sarkar, Sudhirchandra. (Ed.). (2015). *Pouranik Obhidhan.* Kolkata: M.C. Sarkar and Sons Pvt Ltd.

Sen, Amartya. (2005). *The Argumentative Indian*. London: Penguin Books.

.... (2015). *The Country of First Boys.* India: Oxford University Press.

Sharma, Ram Sharan. (1995). *Perspectives in Social and Economic History of Early India.* New Delhi: Munshiram Manoharlal Publishers Pvt Ltd.

Sienkewicz, Thomas J. (2003). *Encyclopaedia of the Ancient World.* Salem Press, page 434.

The Bhagavad Gita. (2009). Sivakasi Tamilnadu, India: Srinivas Fine Arts (P) Ltd.

Williams, Monier M. (2011). *A Sanskrit English Dictionary.* India: Motillal Banaridass Publishers.

Winternitz, M. (1959). *A history of Indian Literature, Part I.* Calcutta: CU, p. 465.

Index

V

W

Y